**John Fawssett** visited his first Greek Islands soon after the end of the Second World War, as a very junior naval officer, when his ship was part of a squadron engaged in clearing live mines from Greek waters.

Subsequent commissions in other warships on station in the Mediterranean led to visits to many parts of Greece including a three day walking expedition among the monasteries of the Mount Athos peninsula.

During a second career in fruit growing he was able, with his wife, to take regular mid-winter motorcaravanning holidays in various parts of the Mediterranean. In 1984 they returned to their home in Sussex after living abroad for three years in their motor caravan, during which time the first edition of this book was researched and written.

**To Wallace Hepburn, lover of the classics.**

# Acknowledgements

A writer of travel guides can hardly be expected to be expert in the interpretation of ancient history. For a general overview I am happy to rely on the writings of Professor A.R. Burn in, amongst others, *The Pelican History of Greece. The Blue Guide: Greece,* compiled by Professor Stuart Rossiter, is an invaluable — if not totally infallible — reference on all manner of archeological and historical matters.

Most islands have a variety of locally printed guide-books on sale: many of them are of doubtful value — at any rate as they present themselves in English translation.

The author and publisher would like to thank the National Tourist Organisation of Greece for their help, and for permission to use the photographs reproduced on the following pages: 8, 11, 15, 20, 24, 37, 65, 77, 64 (lower), 88, 90, 93, 115, 118, 127, 159, 165, 169 (upper), 173, 176. We would also like to thank Mr. D.F. Laoudis of Cares Hydrofoils, for the photograph of the 'Flying Dolphin' (opposite page 128). All other photographs are by the author.

The author would also like to thank Lorna Chaplin for Appendix A (The Greek Language).

**Cover:** A beach on Skiros, just below Skiros town. The same beach can be seen in the background of the photograph showing the statue of Rupert Brooke (page 182).

*Greek Island Series*

# North Aegean Islands

John Fawssett

Skiathos · Skopelos · Thassos
Alonissos · Lemnos · Samothraki
Skiros · Agios Efstratios

**Roger Lascelles,** Cartographic and Travel Publisher
47 York Road, Brentford, Middlesex TW8 0QP   Telephone: 01-847 0935

# Publication Data

| | |
|---|---|
| **Title** | North Aegean Islands |
| **Typeface** | Phototypeset in Compugraphic Times |
| **Photographs** | By the Author and the National Trust Organisation |
| **Printing** | Kelso Graphics, Kelso, Scotland. |
| **ISBN** | 0 903909 74 X |
| **Edition** | First Aug 1984, Second May 1989 |
| **Publisher** | Roger Lascelles |
| | 47 York Road, Brentford, Middlesex, TW8 0QP. |
| **Copyright** | John Fawssett |

# Distribution

| | | |
|---|---|---|
| **Africa:** | South Africa — | Faradawn, Box 17161, Hillbrow 2038 |
| **Americas:** | Canada — | International Travel Maps & Books, P.O. Box 2290, Vancouver BC V6B 3W5. |
| | U.S.A. — | Boerum Hill Books, P.O. Box 286, Times Plaza Station, Brooklyn, NY 11217, (718-624-4000). |
| **Asia:** | Hong Kong — | The Book Society, G.P.O. Box 7804, Hong Kong 5-241901 |
| | India — | English Book Store, 17-L Connaught Circus/P.O. Box 328, New Delhi 110 001 |
| | Singapore — | Graham Brash Pte Ltd., 36-C Prinsep St. |
| **Australasia:** | Australia — | Rex Publications, 413 Pacific Highway, Artarmon NSW 2064. 428 3566 |
| **Europe:** | Belgium — | Brussels - Peuples et Continents |
| | Germany — | Available through major booksellers with good foreign travel sections |
| | GB/Ireland — | Available through all booksellers with good foreign travel sections. |
| | Italy — | Libreria dell'Automobile, Milano |
| | Netherlands — | Nilsson & Lamm BV, Weesp |
| | Denmark — | Copenhagen - Arnold Busck, G.E.C. Gad, Boghallen, G.E.C. Gad |
| | Finland — | Helsinki — Akateeminen Kirjakauppa |
| | Norway — | Oslo - Arne Gimnes/J.G. Tanum |
| | Sweden — | Stockholm/Esselte, Akademi Bokhandel, Fritzes, Hedengrens. Gothenburg/Gumperts, Esselte Lund/Gleerupska |
| | Switzerland — | Basel/Bider: Berne/Atlas; Geneve/Artou; Lausanne/Artou: Zurich/Travel Bookshop |

# Contents

## Part 1: Planning Your Holiday

**1 Why the North Aegean?** 9
The North Aegean Islands 10
Official Information 14

**2 When to go** 17

**3 Getting there** 21
The mainland — where to head for 21
By air to the Greek mainland 22
By rail to the Greek mainland 23
By bus to the Greek mainland 25
By ship to the Greek mainland 25
By road to the Greek mainland 26
Sea transport in the Aegean 28
Departure ports 30 — Island hopping
possibilities 32

**4 Athens and Piraeus** 45
Moving around Athens 45 — City
Centre 48 — Mainline railway
stations 49 — Long distance bus
terminals 50 — Piraeus 51 — airport 53

**5 Accommodation** 56
Hotels 56 — Service flats 56 —
Private houses 57 — Camping 57

**6 Food, drink and entertainment** 59
What to expect 59 — Drinks 61 —
Entertainment 64 — Sports 64

**7 Shopping** 66
Shop opening hours 67 — Books and
newspapers 67 — Currency & banks
67 — Post offices 68 — Telephones 69

**8 Your health and comfort** 70
Medical care 70 — Sunbathing 70 —
Drinking water 71 — Toilets 71

# Part 2: The Islands of the North Aegean

**9 About the North Aegean Islands** 73
Their agriculture 73 — Beaches 74 —
Roads 75 — Moped rental 76 —
Maps and walking excursions 77 —
Highlights of history 78 — Time and
distance 78.

**10 Thassos** 85
Arrival by sea 86 — Road system 89
Centres of population 89 —
Accommodation 94 — Camping 95
— Beaches 97 — Agriculture and
products 99 — Historical background
101 — Cultural interest 103 — Walks
and excursions 104

**11 Samothraki** 109
Arrival by sea 110 — Road system
111 — Centres of population 111 —
Accommodation 113 — Camping 113
Beaches 113 — Agriculture 114 —
Historical background 114 — Walks
and excursions 117

**12 Lemnos** 121
Arrival by air 121 — Arrival by sea
121 — Road system 123 — Centres
of population 124 — Accommodation
126 — Camping 128 — Beaches 128
Agriculture and products 129 —
Historical background 131 — Walks
and excursions 132

**13 Agios Efstratios** 135
Arrival by sea 136 — Roads 137 —
The village 138 — Accommodation
138 — Products 138 — Recreation
139 — History 139 — Tourism 139

# Part 3: The Sporades

**14 Skiathos** 141
Arrival by air 142 — Arrival by sea
142 — Roads 145 — Centres of
population 145 — Accommodation 146
Camping 148 — Beaches 148
Sports 149 — Agriculture 150 —
History 150 — Walks & excursions 152

**15 Skopelos** 155
Arrival by sea 155 — Roads 156
Centres of population 157 — Accom-
-modation 158 — Camping 160
Beaches 160 — Agriculture & products
162 — Historical background 162 —
Walks and excursions 163

**16 Alonissos...and beyond** 167
Arrival by sea 168 — Centres of
population 168 — Accommodation
170 — Camping 170 — Beaches and
excursions 171 — History 171 —
Peristera 172 — Kyra Panagia 172 —
Yioura & Piperi 172 — Psathura 173

**17 Skiros** 175
Arrival by air 176 — Arrival by sea
177 — Roads 177 — Centres of
population 178 — Accommodation 178
— Camping 179 — The countryside 179
— Cultural background 180 — History
181 — Skiros & Rupert Brooke 183

# Appendices

A. The Greek Language 184
B. The Beaufort Conversion Tables 188
C. Useful Conversion Tables 190

# Index

*Old monk of the Greek Orthodox Church. Since its genesis, the Greek Orthodox Church can be perceived running like a continuous thread through the tangled skein of Greek history: a repository for knowledge; a fount of learning; a bulwark of tradition; and a focus for expressions of nationalistic fervour.*

ONE

# Why the North Aegean?

The mate stands above the car-deck, watching the ramp rise like some medieval drawbridge. It shudders to a halt, locking into place. He nods to the seamen beside him on the stern. They bend to release turns of rope from around the bollards, allowing the heavy hawsers to run through the fairleads. The old man on the jetty casts off deftly, and the seamen haul in the heavy ropes. Up on the focsle the capstan clanks into life, straining to raise the long length of rusty anchor chain from the seabed. Slowly the stern is drawn away from the jetty. Islanders wave to friends. Tourist cameras click.

The anchor breaks surface, cascading mud and water, grinding towards its stowage in the hawsepipe. The ferry gathers speed, pulsating to the rhythm of the motors, whilst the jetty recedes.

At last we round the breakwater, heading out into open sea. Sunbeams dance on the gently rippling surface. The waters below become darker, purer, more translucent, slashed by a long scar of boiling white wake, trailing astern. Suddenly the cry of "dolphin" is heard. The ship heels as everyone on deck moves to the same side, anxious to catch a glimpse. A small dark shape can just be seen, suspended for a moment above the surface. Leaping and plunging in harmony, two glistening streamlined brown bodies surge together, speeding towards the ferry, to frolic in the bow-wave, twisting and turning as if to welcome us to their glorious blue Aegean.

For theirs is a special sea, so different from the Ionian Sea that a blindfolded mariner could sense in which he found himself. The characteristics are subtle, and description of them calls for a poet to convey adequacy of expression. But our own senses can absorb them, through an impact of colour, pattern, movement and smell. Sea blending into sky, blue piled upon blues — ever-present frame within which we perceive the islands — islands whose distinctive characters derive from the sea which washes them. Illuminated from above, intense clarity of light vibrant with warmth, dry air as intoxicating as wine. Brown fields, green bushes, sandy beaches — fresh from the palette of the Pantocrator. Fishermen, farmers, patient donkeys, whitewashed dwellings — man truly at peace with Nature.

Only since that time when recorded history began to emerge from myth has our sea been called by its present name. Aegeus, King of Athens, had reluctantly allowed his son Theseus to go to Crete, in hope of slaying the Minotaur. When news of the return of his son's ship was brought to him, the old man hurried to the top of the Acropolis, the sooner to discover for himself the outcome. Greeted by the sight of approaching black sails — agreed signal of death — Aegeus was stricken by such overwhelming grief that he hurled himself from the heights, to drown in the waters below. So the tradition has come down to us, even mentioning the Temple of Athena Nike, close to the entrance gate, as his lookout spot. Although as we stand there today, we may well question the possibility of such a mighty leap.

In those days, the Aegean was already cradle to our eventual European civilization. Ages before — measured within the scale of evolution — man had first arrived to live in settled communities beside the shores of this nameless sea: a sea so docile in summer, so studded with islands, the nearer ones so close. It cannot have been long before some lashed together treetrunks, and paddled themselves across a narrow channel to Thassos. How delighted they must have been to find awaiting them such an hospitable island. And others, lucky men, venturing out from Volos Bay: the first ever to set foot on the golden crescent of Koukounaries beach, and gaze on the delectable beauty all around. No doubt they also were entranced to remain.

## The North Aegean Islands

The islands covered by this book lie in the northern part of the Aegean. Detailed descriptions are given of the eight more important ones, all served by scheduled transport. Some others nearby, less accessible, are also mentioned.

The two most northerly are situated quite close to the Thracian mainland. They are therefore convenient for independent travellers on their way to Turkey, who can easily take the opportunity when passing through Kavala and Alexandroupolis to visit them.

*These pottery plates from Skiros are typical of collections which adorn the walls of island houses.*

**Thassos**

Thassos is extremely beautiful; easily accessible from the mainland opposite, though not from anywhere else. After long experience of welcoming holidaymakers, it now finds itself with a well-developed and harmonious touristic infrastructure, covering a broad range of requirements. Nevertheless, because visitors from northern Europe account for only a small minority, a holiday here has an essentially Greek flavour.

**Samothraki**

Samothraki is impressive, with more grandeur but less beauty than Thassos. The archaeological site continues to be a magnet for lovers of classical antiquities. But a small-scale tourist industry, catering mostly for Greek people, is beginning to emerge independently.

**Lemnos**

Lemnos, the large island in the north west of the Aegean, commands the approaches to the Dardanelles. Its strategic importance is inevitably reflected in a substantial military presence there. Far from the mainland ports of Greece, and lacking access from the much nearer Turkish mainland, the relatively long and expensive journey to Lemnos restricts the number of potential visitors. But that same remoteness has protected the settled way of life of its people — it is this, together with pleasant beaches and a few historical attractions, which helps make the island an agreeable holiday destination. A good choice too for the first or last port-of-call in an island-hopping tour.

**Agios Efstratios**

Agios Efstratios, close to the south of Lemnos, is a small and undeveloped island with a tiny population. Tourists already in Lemnos may wish to make a short visit, though it is of little interest to other holidaymakers.

# The Sporades

Guarding the entrance to the Gulf of Volos lie the islands of the Sporades, which stretch away from the Magnesian Peninsula like uneven links in a broken chain. The word Sporades means scattered or sprinkled, and the name is well-chosen as a glance at their pattern on the map shows. (At one time a much larger grouping of islands, including the present Dodecanese, was also known as Sporades. This practice is perpetuated on some modern maps of German origin, but is no longer correct.) The three main islands of the North Sporades lie close together, forming an homogenous group, well served by sea transport services. Deficient as they may be in historical artefacts, these islands are ideal for those wanting to enjoy the delights of sea, sun, sand and beautiful countryside, undiluted by cultural irrelevances.

## Skiathos

Skiathos, nearest to the mainland, is very attractive, with a profusion of superb sandy beaches. Inevitably there have been substantial tourist developments, which took place over rather a short period, and continue apace. It is from the consequences of this rapid tempo that the few criticisms that might be levelled against the island for a choice of holiday spring.

## Skopelos

Skopelos, more rugged than Skiathos, has considerable tourist development, though perhaps with fewer facilities than some summer visitors could wish for. The majority of the inhabitants carry on their settled and traditional way of life.

## Alonissos

Alonissos was not, until lately, thought of as a holiday destination. But following recent upheavals, few islanders are not now to some extent involved in tourism. The countryside remains quite unspoiled, and the people hope also to hold on to their remaining traditions.

## Skiros

Skiros lies alone far to the south east, as a pendant to the chain of the North Sporades. Its people are proud of their distinctive culture, which is well preserved. Despite the recent opening of an airport its remoteness has hitherto resulted in few developments, as can be seen by the derisory number of hotel beds available. Subject to suitable accommodation being available, the island is well endowed to give the chance of an interesting and unusual holiday experience.

# Official information

**NTOG** The National Tourist Organisation of Greece is known inside Greece as EOT (pronounced like yacht). Its offices answer tourist queries, and hand out a number of free leaflets in several languages. Most of these cover specific areas whereas the one entitled *General Information about Greece* contains a mass of detail useful for planning, which is updated annually. During summer a weekly list of ferries sailing from Piraeus and some other ports is distributed. Mostly the staff are very helpful. NTOG offices relevant to this volume are at: London (195/197 Regent Street W1R 8DRO), Athens, (inside the National Bank of Greece, 1 Karageorgi Servias Street — on a corner of Syntagma); Athens Airport (East); Piraeus; Patras; Igoumenitsa, Thessaloniki, Kavala, Volos; and Evzoni (road frontier). There are also some locally funded tourist offices.

**Place names** The English spelling of Greek place names is a notorious pitfall, since various alternatives in regular use often exist. The versions preferred by NTOG are normally used throughout this book, whilst the more common alternatives are mentioned where appropriate in Part 2. There does in fact exist an Hellenic Standard (ELOT 743) for the transliteration of Greek place names into English. But old habits die hard. For example, in one document professing to observe the standard, the same place name is variously spelt PEIRAIAS (new standard spelling) and PIRAEUS (traditional)!

**Publications** Two useful publications written in English and published monthly, are widely available in Greece. Between them they contain the best available up-to-date travel information — indeed the NTOG weekly sheet originates from one of them. Even so, it cannot be claimed that either is totally comprehensive, particularly for services originating in the provinces and islands. Your friendly Greek travel agent might be persuaded to give you one of his discarded copies.
— *Greek Travel Pages.* Price 550drs. UK representative Timsway Holidays, Nightingales Corner, Little Chalfont, Bucks, HP7 9QS.
— *Key Travel Guide.* Price 250drs. UK representative BAS Overseas Publications Ltd, 48-50 Sheen Lane, London SW14 8LP.

*A tranquil island scene: skiffs idling in the afternoon heat;
fishing nets drying in the sun; white painted houses rising steeply
from the harbour; and amphorae neatly ranged.*

**Tourist police** These police officers are specially selected and trained to deal with tourist problems, to distribute tourist leaflets in places without a NTOG office, and to collect tourist statistics. They are more likely than other police to have some understanding of foreign languages. Until recently they were located in special tourist police stations, but following reorganisation are now ususally found in small sections inside the regular police stations. From Athens they can be contacted directly on the telephone by dialling 171.

## Visas

For those holding a British or Irish passport the entry stamp entitles you to stay for three months. Renewal is a complicated procedure that involves getting a form from a notary, completing it (it is printed in Greek only), buying stamps from another office, providing five passport photographs, evidence that you have changed money and have means of support for the next three months, and generally satisfying the police that you are not working. The length of the extended stay is at the discretion of the police.

TWO

# When to go

The **climate** of the North Aegean is especially favourable to the summer holidaymaker. Between April and September, the sun shines most of the time. April and May, September and the beginning of October are probably the best times to visit. During July and August it is hot — though a lot less hot than on the mainland because of the cooling effects of sea and wind. Average monthly maximum and minimum **temperatures** are shown in table 1.

| Month | THASSOS | | SKIROS | |
|-------|---------|---------|---------|---------|
| | max C° | min C° | max C° | min C° |
| **Jan** | 10.0 | 2.6 | 12.2 | 7.3 |
| **Feb** | 11.0 | 2.4 | 12.8 | 7.6 |
| **Mar** | 13.4 | 4.5 | 13.9 | 8.5 |
| **Apr** | 18.3 | 8.3 | 17.8 | 11.4 |
| **May** | 23.1 | 12.5 | 22.0 | 15.5 |
| **Jun** | 27.7 | 16.7 | 25.9 | 19.1 |
| **Jul** | 30.6 | 18.8 | 27.9 | 21.6 |
| **Aug** | 30.7 | 19.0 | 27.7 | 21.7 |
| **Sep** | 26.4 | 15.6 | 24.4 | 18.7 |
| **Oct** | 21.2 | 11.6 | 20.8 | 15.6 |
| **Nov** | 16.1 | 8.2 | 17.4 | 12.4 |
| **Dec** | 12.5 | 4.6 | 13.8 | 9.2 |

**Table 1:** Average monthly maximum and minimum temperatures (note the remarks under Thassos about the non-typical climate of that island).

There are some distinct differences between the climate of the northern and southern parts of the North Aegean. The north is directly under the influence of the continental landmass, which gives rise to a variable climate more Balkan than Mediterranean. Winters are harsh and cold with high average rainfall and occasionally snow down to sea-level: the summer by contrast is hot and languid, with the mountains of Thrace shielding the coastline, Thassos and to some extent Samothraki from the benevolent effects of the *meltemi*. The word is Turkish, but probably a corruption of the Italian *bel tempo*, meaning good weather. Coming as it does from Central Europe the *meltemi* arrives relatively cool and dry, and thus feels even fresher than it really is.

In the southern part, away from the influence of the mountains, the *meltemi* is able to develop to its full extent. Its season begins fitfully in May and June, becomes fully established during July and August, and diminishes in September and October. The pattern is diurnal, springing up in mid-morning from the NE to reach a peak

| Month | Island | Av. no. of days with measurable rainfall | Av. amt. of rainfall in mm. |
|-------|--------|------------------------------------------|-----------------------------|
| **Jan** | Thassos | 8.6 | 128 |
| | Skiros | 15.8 | 110 |
| **Feb** | Thassos | 7.3 | 109 |
| | Skiros | 11.3 | 70 |
| **Mar** | Thassos | 6.6 | 65 |
| | Skiros | 10.8 | 63 |
| **Apr** | Thassos | 6.0 | 40 |
| | Skiros | 7.3 | 22 |
| **May** | Thassos | 7.1 | 41 |
| | Skiros | 6.2 | 19 |
| **Jun** | Thassos | 4.5 | 31 |
| | Skiros | 3.8 | 9 |
| **Jul** | Thassos | 2.7 | 22 |
| | Skiros | 1.4 | 6 |
| **Aug** | Thassos | 2.3 | 17 |
| | Skiros | 1.5 | 4 |
| **Sep** | Thassos | 3.1 | 49 |
| | Skiros | 3.8 | 18 |
| **Oct** | Thassos | 6.2 | 92 |
| | Skiros | 7.8 | 46 |
| **Nov** | Thassos | 8.0 | 102 |
| | Skiros | 11.0 | 67 |
| **Dec** | Thassos | 9.7 | 166 |
| | Skiros | 15.1 | 109 |

**Table 2:** Average rainfall figures for the most northerly and most southerly islands.

by afternoon, only to die away in the evening. Normally it blows at Force 4-6 on the Beaufort Scale (see Appendix B), but it must be admitted that sometimes it gets out of hand, squalling to Force 7 or even Gale Force 8 occasionally.

Naturally it is the protected beaches to the south and west of islands which feel warmer during the *meltemi* season. But with sea temperatures for swimming there may sometimes be a reverse effect; offshore winds can drive the warm surface water out to sea, which is then replaced by colder water rising up from the depths.

In spring the autumn winds are predominantly from between north east and north west, but there are regular southerly winds as well.

It is worth remembering that the ancient Greeks used to suspend all their deep sea shipping during the six months of winter, because of the danger of sudden and very fierce storms during that period. Winter gales are more often than not from the north east and can be exceptionally severe.

There is an abundance of **rainfall,** but happily for the holidaymaker most of it occurs during the winter months! Moreover, so long as it does not happen on the first day of your holiday, a summer thunderstorm can be an almost welcome interlude! The weather between November and March can be unpleasantly wet and cold, but the islanders endure it on their own. And because of it, these islands are covered with more luxuriant vegetation, and have fewer water supply problems, than elsewhere in the Aegean. Rainfall figures for the most northerly and southerly islands are shown in table 2.

| Jan | Feb | Mar | Apr | May | Jun |
|------|------|------|------|------|------|
| 13.3 | 13.4 | 13.7 | 16.2 | 19.5 | 23.1 |
| **Jul** | **Aug** | **Sep** | **Oct** | **Nov** | **Dec** |
| **25.1** | **25.3** | **23.0** | **19.3** | **15.9** | **13.7** |

**Table 3:** Average seawater (surface) temperatures, for Lemnos.

The sea is quite warm enough for swimming during at least eight months of the year. However, the transition from tepid bathwater to a tingling briskness can come quite suddenly, when an end of summer storm stirs up the sea to its very depths.

*Island communities are great respecters of tradition, particularly in the matter of dress. On most islands the women wear head scarves as a matter of course; the colour and pattern of these varies from island to island. All widows wear black. Elaborate costumes are worn on feast days.*

THREE

# Getting there

Only three of the islands — Lemnos, Skiathos and Skiros — have airports, and it is not possible by means of a scheduled flight to fly direct to any of them (although Skiathos does have a number of charter flights). The other islands can be approached only by sea and, depending on their location, are served by various Greek mainland ports. The first decision for the visitor, therefore, is which mainland departure point to head for. This section deals with that aspect of the journey, and gives general information about these departure points and methods of getting to them. (The second leg — getting from departure point to island — is dealt with in detail in Parts 2 and 3 under the individual island sections — but see also Island hopping possibilities, below.)

## The mainland — where to head for

Modern Greece is a surprisingly centralised society, where practically all political and economic decisions of consequence are made in the capitals — Athens and, to a much lesser extent Thessaloniki. For this reason important dignitaries from the provinces and islands must continually visit them, and so efficient transport links have evolved to meet their needs, and those of the multitude of lesser mortals following in their footsteps.

Athens (followed again at a distance by Thessaloniki), is also by far the easiest part of the mainland of Grece at which to arriv e from abroad. Therefore some detailed information about the capital has been included in this book — how to get there, how to get around and across the city; and how to get out of it again to the point of embarkation for your final destination. But for the convenience of a majority who are unlikely to find it of immediate practical value, much of this detail has been abstracted to the next chapter.

First let us summarise the mainland departure points for the islands:

● For **Thassos:** No airport. The main departure port is Kavala (linked by air to Athens, 2 flights daily); alternative departure port Keramoti.

● For **Samothraki:** No airport. The main departure port is Alexandroupolis (linked by air to Athens, 3 flights daily); a few ferries from Kavala.

● For **Lemnos:** Linked by air to Athens (1 or 2 flights daily) and, alternatively, Thessaloniki (1 flight daily). The main departure port is Kavala (linked by air to Athens); occasional ferries from Kimi, Agios Konstandinos and Piraeus.

● For **Agios Efstratios:** No airport. For most practical purposes travel is via Lemnos (see above); occasional ferries direct from Kimi and Agios Konstandinos.

● For **Skiathos:** Linked by air with Athens (several flights daily) and, alternatively, Thessaloniki (3 flights a week); also by many direct charter flights from abroad. The main departure port is Volos; alternatives are Agios Konstandinos, and, occasionally, Kimi.

● For **Skopelos:** No airport (although onward ferry connection via nearby Skiathos airport is entirely practical). The main departure port is Volos; alternatives are Agios Konstandinos and, occasionally, Kimi.

● For **Alonissos:** No airport (although onward ferry connection via Skiathos airport is practical). The main departure port is Volos; alternatives are Agios Konstandinos and, occasionally, Kimi.

● For **Skiros:** Linked by air with Athens (up to 1 flight daily). The main departure port is Kimi; in summer by hydrofoil from Volos or Agios Konstandinos is a possibility.

# By air to the Greek mainland

### Athens

Scheduled flights arrive in Athens from all over the world. From London (Heathrow) alone there are at least five daily. Flying time is about 3 hours, but a little longer for flights calling first at Thessaloniki or Corfu. There are no longer any flights from regional British airports, but several have scheduled connections via Heathrow or Amsterdam.

In addition, numerous charter flights are provided by tour operators, departing from London and several regional airports.

Seats at very favourable prices are often advertised in the Sunday papers and magazines. Regulations compel such companies selling flight-only seats to provide you with an accommodation voucher for a token payment (e.g. £2), and your flight details will contain an address where this voucher is accepted. But it is understood you are not expected to use it — indeed you could find it is a derelict building if you try to do so.

Athens has one airport (situated at Elenico, about 10kms south of the city centre), split between two completely separate and self-contained sets of terminal buildings. The East (International) terminal, used by all foreign airlines, leads off the main Athens-Glyfada highway. The West terminal, used solely by Olympic Airways for both their domestic and international flights, is alongside the Piraeus-Glifada coast road. Both terminals have a duty-free shop inside the departure building. (See Appendix A for further details.)

**Thessaloniki** From London (Heathrow) there is one direct flight weekly, with flying time 3 hours. There are several direct flights from Dusseldorf, Frankfurt, Munich, Stuttgart, Vienna and Zurich, and less often from Amsterdam, Brussels and Copenhagen.

# By rail to the Greek mainland

Greece can be reached by rail from most European countries. From northern Europe this usually involves joining one of three named expresses:

● Venezia Express (Train 263). Dep Venice 1656, via Belgrade, arr Athens 0800 1½ days later.

● Hellas Express (Train D411). Dep Munich 2138, Zagreb, Belgrade, arr Athens 1330 1½ days later.

● Akropolis Express (Train D291). Dep Munich 0814, route as for Hellas Express, arr Athens 2230 1½ days later.

Travellers from Britain, perhaps the principal users of this book, can connect with any of these trains. Thus the total journey time from London to Athens is at least 2½ days. The cost of the ticket depends on whether the journey is via France, Belgium, or Holland (in order of increasing cost). Details are as follows:

— Dep London (Victoria) 1430 via Dover, Calais, Paris, to Venice; thence by Venezia Express.

— Dep London (Liverpool Street) 1935 via Harwich and the Hook of Holland to Cologne (Köln); thence by Hellas Express.
— Dep London (Victoria) 1300 via Ostend, Köln, to Munich; thence by Akropolis Express.

In practice, since prices for a normal return journey seem rather high (i.e. around £240 second class return) compared with the air fares, rail travel will probably be economic only for people under 26 years of age, entitled to a monthly Inter-rail ticket or the two-monthly Transalpino ticket and senior citizens with British and European rail cards.

*This isolated beach setting is uncommon — most caiques now do their loading in recognised ports, albeit small ones — but vessels like these continue to play an important part in the island transport system. Donkeys and mules remain an essential element of island transport too.*

# By bus

Well established and reputable companies such as Europabus, owned by rail companies, and Eurolines of which National Express is a member, connect Thessaloniki and Athens with most countries of Western Europe. From London there are services most days which can take as little as 2½ days. Prices are of the order of £135 return (1988). Cheaper fares can be found among private operators, some of which have been criticised in the past for inadequate safety standards: moreover the former leader among price cutters, Magic Bus, no longer operates from London.

# By ship to the Greek mainland

Most of the remaining international passenger ships calling at Greek ports now operate as cruise liners. Virtually the only exception are ships run by the Russian Black Sea Company, a few of which call at Piraeus. Thus by far the greater part of passenger capacity now depends on ubiquitous drive-on/drive-off car ferries. Scheduled services, some sensitive to the Near East political situation, give the following possibilities:

| from | between | duration | max. frequency |
|------|---------|----------|----------------|
| Cyprus | Limassol to Piraeus | 31-65 hrs | at least weekly |
| Egypt | Alexandria to Piraeus | 35-57 hrs | weekly |
| Israel | Haifa to Piraeus | 45-59 hrs | several weekly |
| Italy | Ancona to Igoumenitsa | 23-25 hrs | at least daily |
| | Ancona to Patras | 33-36 hrs | at least daily |
| | Bari to Igoumenitsa | 12-14 hrs | daily |
| | Bari to Patras | 18 hrs | daily |
| | Brindisi to Igoumenitsa | 9-10 hrs | several daily |
| | Brindisi to Patras | 15-19 hrs | several daily |
| | Otranto to Igoumenitsa | 9 hrs | several weekly |
| | Venice to Piraeus | 39-40 hrs | at least weekly |
| Syria | Latakia to Piraeus | 78 hrs | occasional |
| | Tartous to Volos | 2½ days | weekly |
| Yugoslavia | Bar to Igoumenitsa | 16 hrs | 2 x weekly |
| | Dubrovnik to Igoumenitsa | 17 hrs | 2 x weekly |

# By road to the Greek mainland

### By private transport

There is no real difficulty in driving across Europe overland to Greece. The easiest route uses the new toll motorway through Austria from Salzburg to Klagenfurt. The main *autoput* (M1/E94E5) through Yugoslavia is joined near Ljubljana. It is a flat and uninteresting road crowded with international juggernauts; much has now been reconstructed to full motorway standards, and new sections are regularly added; but parts of the remainder are in dangerously poor condition, especially north of Belgrade. That stretch can be bypassed by taking the M3 south east from Maribor through Osijek to join a good section of the *autoput* near Sremska Mitrovica — a slower but safer and more interesting route.

The coast road down the Adriatic is even more interesting, but 300kms longer. Being slow and winding, it is also somewhat dangerous. It is not at present possible to transit through Albania, and for political reasons there have sometimes been restrictions on foreign motorists in the province of Kosovo.

Fuel coupons can be bought at the Yugoslav border, for payment in foreign currency. Regulations seem to change in detail from year to year; only recently did it cease to be compulsory for foreigners to use coupons to buy fuel. Currently each coupon has a nominal value of 1300 dinars, but it entitles the motorist to an additional 10 per cent of fuel at standard prices (a complex procedure about which some pump attendants feign ignorance). Unused coupons can be refunded at a border, or through the Automobile Association of Yugoslavia (AMSJ) in Belgrade.

The easier way of getting to Greece is to drive down through Italy and take one of the many car ferries listed above. Those sailing from ports in the 'heel' of Italy (Apulia) should give the cheapest overall journey. Foreign tourists can obtain coupons giving reduced priced for fuel and motorway charges in Italy, either from their national motoring organisations, or from ACI offices at the main entry points.

**Documentation**   Most English-speaking tourists with valid national passports are entitled to a stay of three months. Their vehicles are even more generously treated, since a 'Carnet de Passage en Douanes' is not necessary for periods of up to four months in Greece: instead, an entry is made in the driver's passport at the frontier. Even after four months, a banker's guarantee is an acceptable alternative to the 'Carnet'. An International Driving Permit is not needed by holders of British and several other European national driving licences. But an insurance 'Green Card', valid for Greece, is mandatory. Entry into Greece will be refused if a passport contains the stamp of the Turkish Republic of Cyprus (Kibris).

**Fuel prices** (early 1988) The price of Super (96 octane), at 80dr/litre, is comparable with other countries in the area. Regular seems significantly cheaper, at 75drs/litre, but has the rather low octane value of 90. Diesel at 38dr/litre, is cheap. There is no price discounting, although fuel prices do vary marginally within the country, depending on distance from the refinery. Currently there is no petrol coupons scheme for tourists.

**Motorways** The 'motorway' network, classified as National Road, extends from Evzoni on the Yugoslav border to Thessaloniki and Athens, and from Athens to Patras. The greater part is still single carriageway, although some upgrading work is in progress on busier sections. Some stretches of unimproved main road remain. Driving standards are relaxed, although by convention slower-moving traffic drives on the hard shoulder of single carriageways. Between Evzoni and Athens there are at present three toll sections — the first near Katerini (although another near Thessaloniki can be expected before long) — and two between Athens and Patras. Charges seem modest to foreigners — for example, about £1 for a private car between Evzoni and Athens. Tickets need to be retained for authentication within each toll section.

**Road signs** On main roads the road signs invariably apppear in pairs. The first shows place names using the Greek alphabet, but followed at about 100m by a second in the Roman alphabet. Numerals of course present no difficulty. All other road signs conform generally to normal European conventions. Turnings off towards campsites are almost always signposted from the main road.

**Breakdowns** The Automobile and Touring Club of Greece (ELPA) operates a breakdown service in less remote parts of the country, which is free to foreigners who are members of their own national Automobile or Touring club. Assistance is obtained by dialling 104.

# Sea transport in the North Aegean

The North Aegean is an area where the apparent lack of co-ordinated sea transport network seems particularly irritating to tourists wanting to visit several of the islands. Three of them — Thassos, Samothraki and Skiros — can be approached directly only from mainland ports. Moreover the three main islands of the North Sporades — Skiathos, Skopelos and Alonissos — whilst enjoying excellent internal services, are normally without any direct connections outside. Only from Lemnos are there reasonable onward travel possibilities, via Lesbos and other islands further south; and regrettably the direct service between Lemnos and the North Sporades has in recent years been effectively in abeyance (see Island Hopping Possibilities below). Agios Efstratios, if considered at all, is best thought of as an appendage of Lemnos.

### Shipping companies

The majority of shipping companies serving the North Aegean are small, usually sailing to a single island (or island group), sometimes with only one ship. The main exception is Loucas Nomicos of Piraeus. This company has close connections with the Alkyon Tourist Organisation which, in addition to acting as their agent, has substantial interests in tourism throughout Greece.

Loucas Nomicos operates a fleet of half a dozen modern ships, all car ferries, varying in size between 600 and 2500 tons. (The company continues to own the tiny 250 ton 'Thira', which can with some difficulty find space for up to three cars, but this ferry is currently held in reserve.) In addition to its services in the North Aegean the company also has a route or two operating out of Piraeus. With seven islands in the north to cover, from five mainland ports, using ships of varying capacity, the company is well placed to take advantage of opportunities to optimise its services relative to fluctuating traffic levels, and so tends to make rather frequent timetable changes which may not be widely publicised. The broad framework of the company's operations is entirely clear, and most islands receive an excellent service. But the ordinary tourist can find difficulty working out which departure port will be best for him, the exact days and times of sailing, the ports of call along the route, and the possibilities for onward connection. The information given in Parts 2 and 3, though accurate when written, must be treated with some caution, and local enquiries should certainly be made before travelling. It is another characteristic of Loucas Nomicos to keep their ticket offices exclusive to themselves; only in Kavala does their agent also do business for another company.

The Maritime Company of Lesbos, whose ferries call at Lemnos, is also a substantial operator. But following a fire which destroyed one of its ships, the fleet was reduced to three (Sappho, Omiros and Alcaeos). In any event schedules within the North Aegean represent a minor part of overall operations.

## Flying Dolphins

In 1985 the Ceres Hydrofoil company extended the operations of its "Flying Dolphins" to cover the three main islands of the North Sporades from Volos and Agios Konstandinos. Over a number of years it had been operating a number of Russian built craft in the Saronic Gulf area, where it had built up an enviable reputation for punctuality, reliability and cabin service, its management philosophy having more in common with a small commuter airline than your average Greek shipping company. So when suddenly at Easter two brand new hydrofoils of the latest model first appeared in the Volos area, there was consternation among established ferry operators. They need not have worried too much; for although the hydrofoils are nearly twice as quick as conventional ferries their fares are almost double those of normal third class fares. The hydrofoil has captured those passengers prepared to pay more for a shorter journey; but traffic, especially from people with vehicles, has expanded sufficiently to keep the established operators in business. More recently an additional hydrofoil route between Skiathos and Thessaloniki has been introduced.

Apart from hydrofoils, all the scheduled ferries in the North Aegean are drive-on/drive-off car ferries. Fares are quite reasonable by general European standards, although less of a bargain than they were a decade ago. Small motorcaravans will probably be charged at car rates; minibuses and larger motorcaravans come into a higher price category, probably rating as empty trucks. The exact fare tends to be based on weight, rather than length of the vehicle. The control of loading can seem rather casual; nevertheless car decks often end up very tightly packed indeed. Except on the very largest ferries, vehicles are reversed on board. For this manoeuvre it is usually insisted that all passengers except the driver leave the vehicle.

## By caique

Caiques are essentially locally built fishing boats, but the name covers a wide range of shapes and sizes. Nowadays caiques tend to specialise in fishing, cargo, or tourism. A surprising amount of inter-island cargo is still carried by caique, which in remoter parts still competes on price or flexibility even against drive-on/ drive-off ferries. The captain of such a caique will probably be very pleased to take along a few passengers; from his point of view they pay better than freight — since little or no reduction on the cost of the regular ferry is given — as well as being able to load and unload themselves. He'll probably be agreeable to finding space for motorbikes and bicycles too.

But having confirmed that a caique will eventually be leaving, it's still no easy matter to pin the captain down to a day and time of sailing. Caique captains are often rich men, however scruffy their appearance, and well able to indulge their whims regardless of commercial logic. Caiques may seem to stand half-loaded and deserted for days on end, so frequent visits to check progress are necessary. The place to make enquiries is invariably the café nearest to where the caiques berth.

All this is generally applicable throughout the Aegean. Details of caique routes to the islands of this volume are given in Parts 2 & 3.

## Departure ports

**Alexandroupolis**  844kms from Athens, 334 kms from Thessaloniki, and 44kms from the Turkish border. By road from Yugoslavia the journey is 150kms shorter via Sofia (Bulgaria) and Edirne (Turkey) than through Greece. The capital of Thrace, largely rebuilt since the war. A large, sheltered, underused harbour. Ferries operate from the part nearest the entrance. Ticket offices near the waterfront opposite the entrance. A good campsite on the outskirts (2kms west).

— By rail. 3 services daily from Athens, 4 from Thessaloniki.

— By bus. 4 services daily from Athens, fairly frequent from Thessaloniki.

— By air. Up to 3 flights daily from Athens. Flying time 55 mins. The airport is 7 kms from the town centre.

The bus is quicker than the train, but nowadays costs a lot more (i.e. o/w fare 4330 drs c/f 1995 drs in 1988).

**Kavala** 671kms from Athens, 161kms from Thessaloniki. By road from Yugoslavia the journey is 100kms shorter via Sofia (Bulgaria),

Promahonas (the only Bulgaria-Greece border post) and Drama. The 'de facto' capital of Eastern Macedonia, and an attractive town, especially viewed from seaward. A smallish port, well sheltered and busy. Inter-island ferries leave from the east side, just inside the gates. Thassos ferries leave from a corner of the quayside opposite. Thassos tickets on the quayside; most others from Miliadis, situated inconspicuously on a first floor, between fish market and port gates. Tickets for Agapitos from Alkyon Travel, in the main street near the Tourist Office. Good camp-sites on outskirts both east and west, both with sandy beaches, similar prices, and some traffic noise (Irini, to the east, more used by foreigners).

—By rail. Nearest station is at Drama, services as for Alexandroupolis.

—By bus. Two services daily from Athens, fairly frequent from Thessaloniki.

—By air. Up to 2 flights daily from Athens. The new airport is 32kms from the town centre,

**Keramoti** 45kms south east of Kavala. An alternative departure port for Thassos, giving the shortest crossing. A small municipal campsite on the beach.

**Volos** 316kms from Athens, 204kms from Thessaloniki. The fourth largest town of Greece, and a busy commercial port. Sporades ferries and associated ticket offices are situated centrally on the waterfront, just before the pedestrianised area. There is no longer a commercial airport at Volos. A number of campsites in the Gulf of Volos.

— By rail. 7 services daily from Athens.

— By bus. 9 services daily from Athens. The bus is quicker than the train, but nowadays costs quite a lot more (i.e. o/w 1650 drs c/f 900 drs in 1988).

**Agios Konstandinos** 166kms north of Athens. A very small port facing sheltered water opposite the northern tip of Euboea. The quay is built out directly beside the National Road. The small village, with a ticket office, small hotel, bank, cafes and restaurants, is on the other side of the road.

— By bus. 15 services daily from Athens. In addition a special bus to connect with ferries is run by the Alkyon Tourist Organisation. Departures in Athens from the junction of Psaron and Ag. Pavlou streets (some 300m from Larissis mainline railway station in the direction of Omonia).

**Kimi** A small town on the east coast of Euboea (itself technically an island, but connected to the mainland at Chalkis by a bridge so insignificant that it might easily be overlooked). The port (Paralia Kimi) is substantial and well protected, with hotel and restaurants. Ticket offices on the waterfront, at the end of the jetty.

— By bus. 5 direct services daily from Athens, in addition to more frequent connections involving a change at Chalkis.

— By car. 170kms from Athens. This distance can be shortened by taking one of the internal ferries to Euboea — i.e. from Ag. Marina, north of Marathon to Nea Stira (about every three hours); or from Skala Oropos to Eretria (about every half hour). Approaching the port, the lower road which runs along the coast is in very poor condition. It is better to take the upper road which runs through the town high above.

# Island hopping possibilities

The general structure of passenger shipping in the North Aegean has already been discussed (under Sea Transport in the North Aegean), and further details concerning individual islands are given in Parts 2 and 3. But many readers will be interested in planning journeys to other islands, using scheduled ferries. Reliable information about some of these is not easy to come by. It is true that the NTOG weekly sheet has lately become increasingly comprehensive; even so, its layout makes it difficult to form a coherent picture.

Reference has already been made to the peculiar problems of island hopping within the North Aegean. Only Lemnos is a suitable springboard for continuing beyond, with its direct connections to Lesbos, Chios, Samos and Rhodes (amongst others), which then permit further travel to the Cyclades, Crete and other islands of the Dodecanese. For travellers visiting Thassos and Samothraki it is not difficult to get to Lemnos via Kavala. But from the North Sporades, although a ticket can theoretically be bought there, in practice the ferry normally makes the trip to Lemnos from Agios Konstandinos or the Euboean port of Kimi, which would require a tedious indirect voyage.

Virtually all Greek islands of any importance now have a car ferry service, relied on as the chief means of bringing in goods and for transporting foot passengers — even if tourist motorcars are not carried to a few islands. A diminishing number of passenger-only

## TRANSPORT LINKS
### (Islands except Sporades)

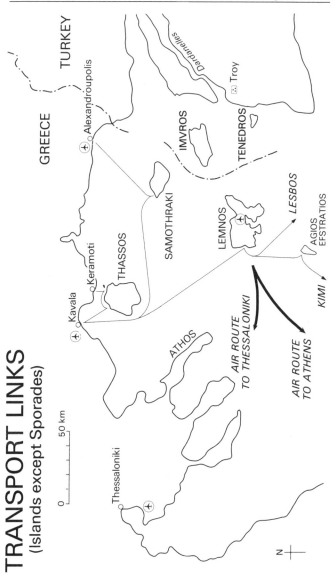

ships still operate, but the tendency is for them to be replaced by car ferries or hydrofoils. There has also been a trend for some ferries operating out of Piraeus to move away from the congestion there to smaller ports elsewhere which sometimes shortens distances as well.

Where islands lie close to one another, in relation to their distance from the mainland port, fairly logical networks have evolved within those groups. But intending passengers should be aware of the following factors.

— Islanders themselves have usually little interest in visiting other islands, unless perhaps for some important festival (when special services will be laid on). Otherwise they want to get to the mainland as quickly as possible. This requirement is, of course, quite opposite to that of an island-hopping tourist, but has naturally had more influence on the planning of schedules. Island ports often alternate with mainland ones, regardless of prolonging the time between islands.

— With few exceptions, local operators make little effort to publicise their services. Timetables, where found, probably list sailings by ship's name rather than the operating company. Destinations are often given as ports, sometimes with obscure names, rather than islands.

— Shipping companies, all of them privately owned, need to have their route licences renewed annually by the Ministry of Mercantile Marine. Established operators are unlikely to be disturbed, but marginal ones bidding for fringe routes — those which sometimes provide vital links in island-hopping chains — may have little idea until late in the previous year which, if any, they are going to be allocated. Bankruptcies, leading to an unexpected termination of services, are not uncommon; nor is it unknown for a route to be suspended in low season, whilst waiting for traffic levels to improve.

— Modern ferries are required to conform to specifications suitable for troop-carrying duty in an emergency — the evacuation of PLO fighters from Tripoli in 1983 was a recent example. But this does explain the apparently casual attitude to passenger comfort in some cases.

— Regardless of their size, or the willingness of their captain, no Greek ferry is officially permitted to put to sea when winds of Force 9 on the Beaufort Scale are forecast. (See Appendix B.) It is therefore advisable to have a margin in reserve before your flight home departs: thus diversions such as climbing the Acropolis might best be left until the end of your holiday.

# THE SPORADES-
# TRANSPORT LINKS

## LEGEND FOR ISLAND MAPS

| | | |
|---|---|---|
| Road (Tarmac) | Principal Beach | |
| Road (Unsurfaced) | Hotel | H⊙ |
| Mule Track | Monastery | M⊙ |
| Car Ferry | Church | |
| Airport | Archaeological site | |

— Services between Greek islands and the Turkish mainland are very sensitive to fluctuations of tension between the two countries. Sailings may not actually cease, but operators are liable to keep a very low profile — so that reliable information is hard to come by even in the departure port. In any event, fares are very high in relation to the short distances involved; and for obscure reasons inward and outward bound prices can differ.

## Classes

Hydrofoils and short distance ferries are effectively single class: but on the longer distance ships there may be up to four classes:

● First Class. The standard varies from boat to boat, but you are generally paying for seclusion. The fare is about four times that of third class and, where there is a choice, works out dearer than flying the same route.

● Second Class. Use of upholstered bench-type seats which are comfortable for a snooze. Twice the fare of third class.

● Tourist Class. Individual seats, sometimes reclining, in long rows. Fifty per cent more expensive than third class.

● Third or Deck Class. Your freedom is confined to the upper decks. There will be some slatted wooded benches, but these easily get dirty with salt or even soot. Even if you can find space to flake yourself down on a beach mat or sleeping bag, you run the risk of sunburn by day and hypothermia by night. Nevertheless, you do get remarkable value for your money. There is sometimes a hot shower to be found on the upper deck so it's worth having a towel and toiletries with you.

A more egalitarian system usually prevails out of season. The first class lounge is kept locked, unless some VIP is travelling: everyone else buys a third class ticket, and uses the tourist lounge.

**Footnote Hydrofoils:** in addition to its North Sporades service, the Ceres company operates a substantial network, based on Piraeus, to the islands of the Saronic Gulf (extending in summer to Kythira and the Gulf of Nauplion). Their earlier service in the Cyclades is suspended, though it may possibly reopen on an all-the-year-round basis. Kouros Travel runs a summer-seasonal network in the Dodecanese, based on Rhodes; services are mostly to Kos, also to Patmos, Leros and Symi (though the smaller island destinations seem to vary from year to year). An Ionian service from Patras to Kefallonia and Zakynthos was discontinued when its operator, Alkyonis Speed Boats, transferred his two hydrofoils to the Dodecanese, combining forces with Kouros Travel.

*An old man in traditional costume leads his donkey slowly down a narrow street. This one, and fortunately many others in the town, are quite unsuited to use by motorcars.*

## Table of inter-island connections

The information contained in the table on the following pages has been assembled to assist in the planning of economical island-hopping sequences. It is based on car ferry services only; naturally foot passengers can enjoy additional mobility by taking passenger ships, hydrofoils (see footnote) and caiques. The islands not listed are either of little tourist importance, or else tourist motor vehicles cannot be disembarked there.

Under each island the following information is shown: alternative ports liable to be given as destinations; normal mainland departure ports; journey times; maximum weekly frequencies; other islands which can be reached directly, as first port of call; international connections. Naturally, since the underlying data are continually changing, confirmation needs be sought locally.

The following example should help to make things clear: Chios (Eastern Aegean Group). Alternative island port, Mesta. Mainland departures from Piraeus, 10 hours, frequent (i. e. more than 7) sailings each week; from Kavalla, 16 hours, 1 sailing weekly; and from Thessaloniki, duration uncertain, 1 sailing weekly. From Chios there are direct sailings to Lesbos, 4 hours, more than 7 weekly; to Samos, 3 hours, 1 weekly; to Psara, 4 hours, 4 weekly; and to Oinoussa, 1 hours, 6 weekly. There is an international sailing to Cesme, 1 hour, with more than 7 sailings weekly.

**Key to Table.** CY = Cyclades, DO = Dodecanese, E = East Aegean, IO = Ionian, N = North Aegean, SA = Saronic, SP = Sporades.
Numbers in brackets represent the approximate duration in hours of the quickest journey. Other numbers are for frequency in high season, whilst f indicates at least 7 services each week.
? indicates there are some doubts as to reliability of data, although a connection is thought probable.

| Island destination | Mainland departure | Other islands reached directly | International connections |
|---|---|---|---|
| Aegina (SA) (Ag Marina) | Piraeus (1) f Methana (¾) f | Poros (1¾) f | |
| Alonissos (SP) | Volos (5½) f Ag. K'standinos(6)3 Kimi (2½) 3 | Skopelos (½) f | |
| Amorgos (CY) (Egiali) (Katapola) | Piraeus (?) 4 | Paros (3) 1 Astipalea (3) 2 Donoussa (1½) 2 Koufonissia (1) 3 | |
| Anafi (CY) | Piraeus (?) 1 | Thera (1) 1 | (?cars landed?) |
| Andros (CY) (Gavrion) | Rafina (3) 6 | Tinos (2½) 6? | |
| Antikythira | Piraeus (18) 2 Gythion (7) 2 | Kythira (1) 2 Crete (3) 2 | |
| Astipalea (CY) | Piraeus (16) 2 | Amorgos (3) 2 Kalymnos (3) 1 Donoussa (4) 1 | |
| Chios (E) (Mesta) | Piraeus (10) f Kavala (16) 1 Thessaloniki (12) 1 | Lesbos (4) f Samos (3) 2 Oinoussa (1¾) 6 Psara (4½) 4 | Cesme (1) f |
| Corfu (IO) (Kerkyra) | Igoumenitsa (1½)f Patras (11½) f | Paxi (2) 3 | Brindisi (8) f Bar (13) 2 Bari (10) 6 Dubrovnik (15) 4 Otranto (7) 5 + |
| Crete Chania Heraklion Kastelli Sitia | Piraeus (11) f Piraeus (11½) f Gythion (4) 2 Thessaloniki (12)1 | Shinoussa (7) 1 Naxos (8) 2 Antikythira (3) 2 Kassos (3) 2? Thera (5) 6 | Limassol (27) 2 Haifa (43) 2 |
| Donoussa (CY) | Piraeus (12) 2 | Astipalea (4) 1 Naxos (2) 1 Amorgos (2) 2 | (?cars landed?) |

| Island destination | Mainland departure | Other islands reached directly | International connections |
|---|---|---|---|
| Folegandros (CY) | Piraeus (12) 1 | Sikinos (1) 1<br>Thera(3) 1 | (?cars landed?) |
| Ikaria (E)<br>(Ag. Kirikos)<br>(Evdilos) | Piraeus (10) f | Syros (4½) 1<br>Paros (4½) 4<br>Samos (2) f | |
| Ios (CY) | Piraeus (9) 4 | Naxos (2) 4<br>Sikinos (1) 1<br>Thera (3) 4 | |
| Ithaca (IO)<br>(Vathy)<br>(Frikes) | Patras (6) f<br>Astakos (2) f<br>Vassiliki (4) f | Kefallonia (1) f<br>Paxi (5) 1 | |
| Kalymnos (DO) | Piraeus (14) f | Kos (2) f<br>Leros (1½) 5<br>Astipalea (3) 1 | |
| Karpathos (DO) | | Kassos (1) 2?<br>Khalki (3) 2? | |
| Kassos (DO) | | Crete (3) 2?<br>Karpathos (1) 2? | |
| Kea (CY) | Lavrion (1) f | Kythnos (2) 3 | |
| Kefallonia (IO)<br>(Poros)<br>(Sami)<br>(Fiskardo)<br>(Ag. Efemia)<br>(Argostoli) | Killini (1½) f<br>Patras (3½) f<br>Igoumenitsa (5) 3<br>Vassiliki (1½) f<br>Astakos (3) f | Ithaca (1) f<br>Zakinthos (2) 1 | Brindisi (14) 3 |
| Khalki (DO) | | Karpathos (3) 2?<br>Rhodes (3) 2? | |
| Kimolos (CY) | Piraeus (11) 2 | Milos (2) 2<br>Syros (4) 2<br>Sifnos (2) 1 | |
| Kos (DO) | Piraeus (16) f | Kalymnos (2) 6<br>Rhodes (4½) 6<br>Nissiros (2) 1 | Bodrum (½) ? |
| Koufonissia(CY) | Piraeus (12) 3 | Shinoussa (1) 3<br>Amorgos (1) 3 | |

| Island destination | Mainland departure | Other islands reached directly | International connections |
|---|---|---|---|
| Kythira (Ag. Pelagia) (Kapsali) (Platia Ammos) | Piraeus (11) 2 Neapolis (1) 5 Gythion (2½) 2 | Nil | |
| Kythnos (CY) | Lavrion (2) 3 Piraeus (3½) 4 | Serifos (2) 4 Kea (2) 3 | |
| Lemnos (E) (Myrina) (Kastro) | Kavala (5) 4 Piraeus (60) 1 Ag. K'standinos (10) 1 Kimi (5½) 1 | Lesbos (6) f Ag.Efstratios (2)2 | |
| Leros (DO) | Piraeus (12) 5 | Kalymnos (1½) 5 Patmos (1½) 5 | |
| Lesbos (E) (Mytilini) | Kavala (14) 2 Piraeus (13) f Thessaloniki (16)1 | Chios (4) f Lemnos (6) f | Dikeli (2) ? |
| Milos (CY) | Piraeus (9) 3 | Kimolos (2) 2 Sifnos (2) 3 | |
| Mykonos (CY) | Piraeus (6) 3 Rafina (5) 5? | Tinos (1) f? | (?cars landed?) |
| Naxos (CY) | Piraeus (6) f | Paros (1) f Crete (8) 2 Donoussa (1½) 1 Ios (2) 4 | |
| Nissiros (DO) | Piraeus (16) 1 | Kos (2) 1 Tilos (1) 1 | (?cars landed?) |
| Oinoussa (E) | | Chios (1¾) 6 | |
| Paros (CY7 | Rafina (5½) 3 Piraeus (6½) f | Ikaria (4½) 4 Amorgos (3) 1 Naxos (1) f Syros (2) f | |
| Patmos (DO) | Piraeus (10) 5 | Leros (1½) 5 Syros (6) 1 | |
| Paxi (IO) | Patras (10) 1 | Corfu (2) 3 Ithaca (5) 1 | |

| Island destination | Mainland departure | Other islands reached directly | International connections |
|---|---|---|---|
| Poros (SA) | Methana (½) f<br>Galatas (5mins) f<br>Piraeus (3) f | Aegina (1¾) f | |
| Psara (E) | | Chios (4½) 4 | |
| Rhodes (DO) | Piraeus (15 + ) f | Khalki (3) 2?<br>Kos (4½) 6<br>Symi (2) 1 | Limassol (14) 4<br>Marmaris (2) ?<br>Latakia (55) 1<br>Haifa (28) 1<br>Alexandria (39) 1 |
| Salamis (SA) | Perama (10mins) f<br>Perama (Megara)(¼) f | Nil | |
| Samos (E)<br>(Vathy)<br>(Karlovasi) | Piraeus (12) f | Ikaria (2) f<br>Chios (3) 2 | Kusadasi (2) f |
| Samothraki (N) | Alexandroupolis (3) f<br>Kavala (4) 1 | Nil | |
| Serifos (CY) | Piraeus (5) 4 | Kithnos (2) 4<br>Sifnos (1) 2 | |
| Shinoussa (CY) | Piraeus (12) 3 | Crete (7) 3<br>Koufonnissia (1) 3 | (?cars landed?) |
| Sifnos (CY)<br>(Apollonia) | Piraeus (6) 4 | Milos (2) 3<br>Serifos (1) 4<br>Kimolos (2) 1 | |
| Sikinos (CY) | Piraeus (11) 1 | Ios (1) 1<br>Folegandros (1) 1 | (?cars landed?) |
| Skiathos (SP) | Volos (3) f<br>Ag. K'dinos (3) f<br>Kimi (4½) 3 | Skopelos (1) f<br>Lemnos ? | |
| Skiros (SP) | Kimi (2) f | | |
| Skopelos (SP) | Volos (4) f<br>Ag. K'dinos (4) f<br>Kimi (3½) 3 | Alonissos (½) f<br>Skiathos (1) f | |

| Island destination | Mainland departure | Other islands reached directly | International connections |
|---|---|---|---|
| Symi (DO) | Piraeus (18) 1 | Tilos (2) 1<br>Rhodes (2) 1<br>Patmos (6) 1 | |
| Syros (CY) | Piraeus (4½) f<br>Rafina (3½) 3 | Ikaria (4½) 1<br>Kimolos (4) 1<br>Paros (2) f<br>Tinos (1) 4 | |
| Thassos (N)<br>(Prinos) | Kavala (1) f<br>Keramoti (½) f | Nil | |
| Thera (CY)<br>(Santorini)<br>(Oia) | Piraeus (12) 5 | Anafi (2) 1<br>Ios (3) 4<br>Folegandros (3) 1<br>Crete (5) 6 | |
| Tilos (DO) | Piraeus (16) 1 | Nissiros (1) 1<br>Symi (2) 1 | (?cars landed) |
| Tinos (CY) | Rafina (5½) 6<br>Piraeus (4½) 3 | Andros (2½) 6<br>Mykonos (1) f?<br>Syros (1) 4 | |
| Zakinthos (IO) | Killini (1) f | Kefallonia (2) 1 | |

**Note:** Euboea and Levkas, both technically islands, but with bridge or chain-ferry road connection, have been treated as if part of the mainland.

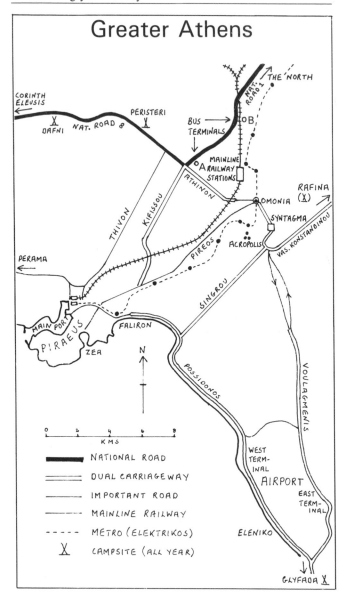

FOUR

# Athens and Piraeus

## Greater Athens

Like most capitals, Athens can seem vast and confusing to the first time visitor. It is certainly true that the modern city sprawls over a huge area, and that some 3.3 million people — one third of the total population of the country — live there. But the tourist passing through needs only to think in terms of the city centre and his arrival and departure points — be they by ship, rail, bus or aeroplane. Thus there are five areas of interest:

- Athens, city centre.
- Athens, main line railway stations.
- Athens, long distance bus terminals.
- Piraeus, port of Athens.
- Athens airport, at Elinco.

This chapter considers how to move around within Greater Athens, describes the five areas above, and suggests the best ways of travelling between them.

## Moving around Athens

**Taxis** These are plentiful and relatively cheap. However, because of regulations introduced to lessen smog in the city, private motor cars can only be used on alternate days — according to whether their registration ends with an odd or even number. Consequently car owners must find an alternative method of getting to work — and so many appropriate the taxis.

On the other hand it's quite in order to stop any passing taxi with an empty seat that seems to be going in the right direction, and ask to be taken along. You still have to pay as if you had the taxi all to yourself, thus drivers tend to be more enthusiastic about sharing than your fellow passengers. Few drivers are proficient in foreign

languages, and the official tariff is complicated; so it can happen
that both the place the driver expects you to get out and the fare
he demands can come as disagreeable surprises. Even so, taxis —
if you can obtain one — may well be faster and more convenient
than other public transport, even if more expensive.

**Buses** The metropolitan network is run by three independent
operators, whose activities are co-ordinated by the supervising
authority OAS. Buses come in all colours of the rainbow, each
having its own significance. Ordinary city buses belong to EAS, are
coloured **blue**, and normally function between 0500 and midnight.
Fares are a flat 30 drs per journey irrespective of distance. Frequent
checks are made by uniformed inspectors, so tickets need to be kept,
but early morning travel before 0800 is free. The **green** bus service
differs from the blue only in that it is run by ISAP, whose main
function is organising the underground railway. **Orange** buses go
ouside Athens to other towns within Attica. There are also **yellow
trolley** buses, which mostly circulate within the centre, operated by
ILPAP. These are not to be confused with the **yellow (express)**
buses, relatively few in number, but important for tourists because
they go from the airport to the city centre and Piraeus. Their fare
is a flat 100 drs (150 drs between midnight and 0600), but journeys
are faster because of fewer intermediate stops; they also have space
specially set aside for luggage.

In the summer of 1988 a new Express Bus Service was introduced,
linking the two Long Distance Bus Terminals with the Airport, via
the City Centre and Railway Stations. They are double deckers, of
a type well known to Londoners, but painted blue and white with
a yellow stripe. Line A starts from Bus Terminal A, Line B from
Bus Terminal B. Those going to the Airport West (Olympic
Airways) carry a diagonal red stripe across the A or B on their
destination indicator: those for the Airport East (International) have
a plain A or B.

Athenians are enthusiastic bus users, so their buses are often
crowded. Another difficulty for the foreigner is to work out which
route number to take. These are listed at the bus stops (*stasis*),
together with their destinations — but naturally in Greek.

**Underground railway** A single route electric railway connects the
north east suburb of Kifissia with Piraeus, via the city centre.
Mostly it runs on the surface, though like the district lines in
London, it does dive underground below the city centre. Athenians

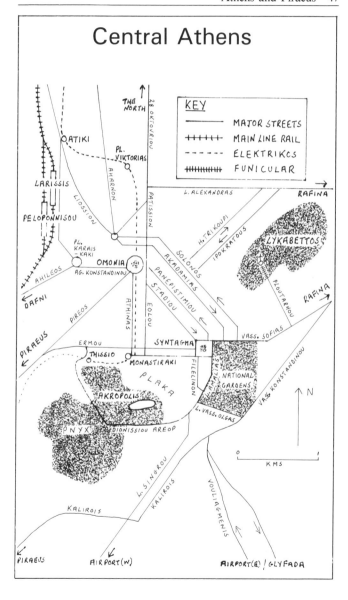

call it the *elektrikos,* and Metro is also understood. Fares are 30 drs, as on the blue buses, and because ticket offices do not open until 0800, have likewise come to be regarded as free until that time. But increasingly stations are being automated; first you buy your ticket from a coin machine, then you must insert it into an automatic turnstyle — a tricky operation, so it may be best to stand aside and watch a local do it. Trains run between 0500 and midnight, about every 5 minutes on the section between Omonia and Piraeus (every 15 mins north of Omonia). Two new intersecting lines are at present under construction.

If there's a station near where you want to go, the Metro usually offers the quickest and most comfortable journey. Omonia in the centre, Monastiraki further south adjoining Plaka, and Thission, for the Acropolis, are stations useful to the tourist.

# Athens, city centre

**Orientation** The city centre can be regarded — by today's tourist as it was by the ancient Greeks — as that area lying between the **Acropolis** and **Lykabettus.** These two hills are invaluable for orientation, since one or both can be seen from most parts. From both an enormous blue and white national flag of Greece flutters in any breeze. The Acropolis, with Parthenon on top, is too well known to need description. Lykabettus is taller and slighter, even more conspicuous as a landmark, and topped by the white chapel of St George.

The central area is quite small and compact; and thanks to those Bavarian town planners who arrived with King Otto (the first King of Greece) in 1834, its street layout is perfectly logical. Midway between Lykabettus and the Acropolis is **Syntagma** (Constitution Square), one of the two great central concourses, near which are many important buildings housing government, business and organisations (such as airlines and hotels) of interest to the tourist. A pair of wide streets leaves it towards the north west, only to converge again after precisely 1 km at **Omonia**, the second great concourse, and centre of commercial life of Athenians and many tourists too. Roads fanning out from Syntagma and Omonia lead to all destinations of interest to tourists.

The Olympic Airways office stands on the south side of Syntagma. Round the corner, at the top of Amalias, is the British Airways office.

### Transport connections

● **To the airport (East, International).** Double decker Express bus Lines A and B (plain only) every 20 mins from Omonia and Syntagma (every hour between midnight and 0600). Also blue bus 121 every 20 mins from Vassilis Olgas (third turning left down Amalias).

● **To the airport (West).** Double decker Express buses from Omonia and Syntagma (only those carrying a diagonal red stripe across the A or B on their destination indicator). Olympic Airways bus every half hour from outside their office (100 drs). Also blue bus 133 every half hour from near the same point, or blue bus 122 every 20 mins from Vassilis Olgas.

● **To the mainline railway stations.** Double decker Express bus Line B (plain or diagonal red stripe). Yellow trolley bus 1 every 10 mins from 0500 to midnight from Amalias, opposite the British Airways office, or Omonia.

● **To the long distance bus terminals.** To Terminal A (100 Kifissou St), double decker Express bus Line A (plain or diagonal red stripe), and blue bus 051 every 15 mins (every 40 mins from midnight to 0500) from Menandrou/Vilara, near Omonia. To Terminal B (260 Liossion St), double decker Express bus Line B (plain or diagonal red stripe), and blue bus 024 from Amalias and Omonia.

● **To Piraeus.** First choice is by *elektrikos* from Omonia. Green bus 040 runs every 10 minutes day and night from Filellion Street/Syntagma (near Olympic Airways office), but is best avoided during the rush hour. Buses from many other parts.

# Athens, mainline railway stations

The two Athens railway stations are situated close together, about 1km north west of Omonia. Larissis, nearer to the centre, is the terminus for services from northern Greece, and indeed from the rest of Europe. About 200m beyond is Peloponissou, serving the Peloponnese: trains actually start at Piraeus, and run on a narrower 1 metre guage. Note that all the long distance buses operated by OSE (the State railway) to destinations such as Thessaloniki, Alexandroupolis, Corinth and Patras, leave from outside their appropriate station.

**Transport connections**

● **To the city centre,** double decker Express bus Line B (plain or diagonal stripe) every 20 mins (every hour between midnight and 0600), and Yellow trolley bus 1 every 10 mins from 0500 to midnight to Omonia and Syntagma/Amalias.

● **To the airport (East, International).** Double decker Express bus Line B (plain only).

● **To the airport (West, Olympic Airways).** Double decker Express bus Line B (red diagonal stripe only).

● **To the long distance bus terminals.** For Terminal A, probably safer via the City Centre. For Terminal B double decker Express bus Line B (plain or red diagonal stripe).

● **To Piraeus.** A train from Peloponissou would be convenient, but they are not frequent. Otherwise via Omonia and the *elektrikos,* or Syntagma (Filellion Street and green bus 040).

# Athens, long distance bus terminals

Apart from the OSE buses (see railway stations above), most long distance buses in Greece are run by a pool of operators known as KTEL. In Athens they use two termini some 3 kms from the centre, convenient to the motorways. **Terminal A at 100 Kifissou Street**, close to the motorway to Patras, serves the Peloponnese together with a majority of more distant destinations. **Terminal B at 260 Liossion Street**, near the motorway to Thessaloniki and 2 kms north of Terminal A, serves nearer destinations in the eastern half of central Greece.

**Transport connections.**
● from Terminal A. Double decker Express bus Line A, plain to the East Airport, red diagonal stripe to the West. For Piraeus, change at City Centre (Omonia or Syntagma). Alternatively blue bus 051 to Omonia then change.
● from Terminal B. Double decker Express bus Line B, plain to the East Airport, red diagonal stripe to the West. For Piraeus, change at City Centre (Omonia or Syntagma). Alternatively blue bus 024 to Amalias then change.

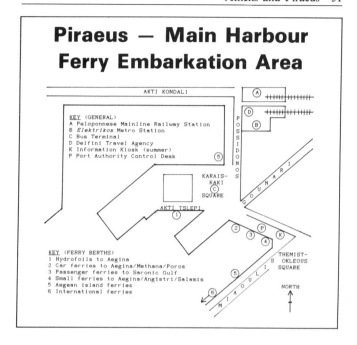

# Piraeus — Main Harbour Ferry Embarkation Area

AKTI KONDALI

KEY (GENERAL)
A Peloponnese Mainline Railway Station
B *Elektrikos* Metro Station
C Bus Terminal
D Delfini Travel Agency
K Information Kiosk (summer)
P Port Authority Control Desk

KARAIS-
KAKI
SQUARE

AKTI TSLEPI

KEY (FERRY BERTHS)
1 Hydrofoils to Aegina
2 Car ferries to Aegina/Methana/Poros
3 Passenger ferries to Saronic Gulf
4 Small ferries to Aegina/Angistri/Salamis
5 Aegean island ferries
6 International ferries

THEMIST-
OKLEOUS
SQUARE

NORTH

## Piraeus, port of Athens

With the exception of most hydrofoils which use Zea, all scheduled Aegean island ferries leave from the east side of the main harbour. Their approximate departure areas are marked (5) on the harbour map, which also shows the locations of the two railway stations (Peloponissou (A) and *elektrikos* (B)) and the main bus terminal (C).

Along the waterfront there seem to be innumerable tourist offices (*practórios*), each competing furiously to attract your custom — the greatest concentration beside the bus terminal. Any of them can sell you a valid ticket at the correct price; but few of them represent all the operators, nor can most be bothered to explain all the possibilities or how to get to the departure point. One of the exceptions is the charming owner of Delfini Travel(D) (recently renamed M Chondrocoucis), which is situated inside the *elektrikos* station (in the far right hand corner as you get off the train).

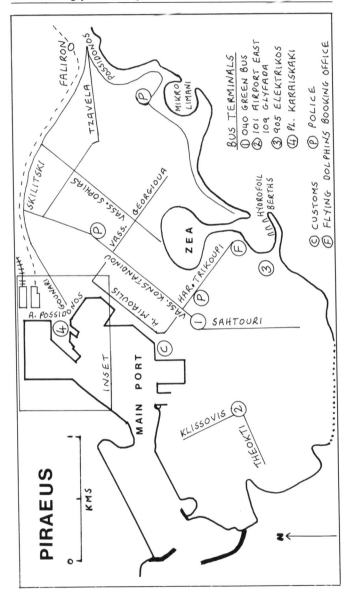

PIRAEUS

BUS TERMINALS
① 040 GREEN BUS
② 101 AIRPORT EAST
   109 GLYFADA
③ 905 ELEKTRIKOS
④ PL. KARAISKAKI
Ⓟ POLICE
Ⓕ FLYING DOLPHINS BOOKING OFFICE
Ⓒ CUSTOMS

MAIN PORT
INSET
ZEA
MIKRO LIMANI
HYDROFOIL BERTHS

FALIRON
POSSIDONOS
TZAVELA
SKILITSKI
VASS. SOPHIAS
VASS. GEORGIOUA
VASS. KONSTANDINOU
HAR. TRIKOUPI
A. MIAOULIS
A. POSSIDONOS
GOUNAKI
SAHTOURI
KLISSOVIS
THEOKTI
KMS

Another possible source of advice in summer is the information kiosk (Inset K). Tourist police also patrol the area in summer. At other times you might try the Port Authority control desk (Inset P), but the official may not speak English, even if he has the time.

### Transport connections

● City centre. First choice is the *elektrikos*. Outside the rush hour green bus 040 to Filellion Street (Syntagma) leaving every 10 minutes day and night from Sakhtouri Street (1). Many buses to other parts.

● To the airport (East, International). Yellow express bus 19 from Akti Tselepi (Inset 1, the south side of shipping offices block on Karaiskaki Square) every 15 mins from 0600 to midnight (and every half hour from midnight to 0600). Also blue bus 101 from Klissovis/Theotaki (2).

● To the airport (West, Olympic Airways). Yellow express bus 19 on its way to the airport (East) — see above. Also blue bus 109 every 20 mins from Klissovis/Theotaki (2).

● To the mainline railway stations. By train from Peloponissou station (A), if there's one running. Otherwise via the city centre — Omonia (*elektrikos*) or Syntagma (green bus 040), then change.

● To long distance bus terminals. Via city centre, then change.

# Athens airport

Athens has one airport (situated at Elenico, about 10 kms south of the city centre), split between two completely separate and self-contained sets of terminal buildings. The East (International) terminal, used by all foreign airlines, leads off the main Athens-Glyfada highway. The West terminal, used exclusively by Olympic Airways for both their domestic and international flights, is alongside the Piraeus-Glyfada coast road. Both terminals have a duty free shop inside the departure building.

There is a tunnel under the runway to connect the two terminals, but it has not been used for passengers since airports became vulnerable to international terrorism. Transfer between the two terminals is now by bus, running outside the perimeter fence, i.e.:

● Piraeus yellow express bus 19 every 15 mins from 0600 to 2000 (every half hour from midnight to 0600), from the Airport (East).

● Olympic Airways shuttle bus (free to O.A. passengers), leaving the West Airport every hour on the hour, and the East Airport every hour on the half-hour.

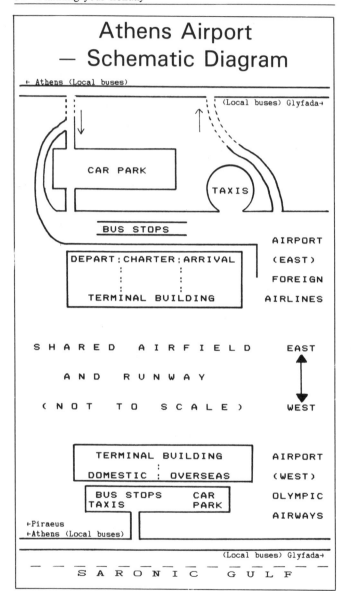

# Athens Airport
# — Schematic Diagram

← Athens (Local buses)

(Local buses) Glyfada→

CAR PARK

TAXIS

BUS STOPS

| DEPART | CHARTER | ARRIVAL |

TERMINAL BUILDING

AIRPORT
(EAST)
FOREIGN
AIRLINES

S H A R E D   A I R F I E L D

A N D   R U N W A Y

( N O T   T O   S C A L E )

EAST

WEST

TERMINAL BUILDING

DOMESTIC : OVERSEAS

BUS STOPS   CAR
TAXIS       PARK

←Piraeus
←Athens (Local buses)

AIRPORT
(WEST)
OLYMPIC
AIRWAYS

(Local buses) Glyfada→

S A R O N I C   G U L F

**Athens Airport (East)** The impressive-looking terminal was designed by the Finnish-American Eero Saarinen — he was also responsible for the American Embassy in Grosvenor Square, London, Unfortunately it has difficulty coping in high summer, among other reasons because of the many tourists who doss down in public spaces whilst waiting for late night flights. Arrivals are usually easier: but whilst waiting to pick up your luggage do not miss the chance to ask for advice or leaflets from the NTOG information desk — once past customs you'll not be able to go back there, nor to the equally helpful Olympic Airways information desk.

The terminal building is in three sections — arrivals, departures and between them, charters. Outside the arrivals building a taxi rank stands directly opposite. On the left is the airport bus terminal:

● To the city centre. Double decker Express bus A or B (plain) every 20 mins to Syntagma & Omonia (every hour between midnight & 0600). Also blue bus 121 every 20 mins to Vassilis Olgas.

● To the mainline railway stations. Double decker Express bus Line B (plain) every 20 mins.

● To the long distance bus terminals. For Terminal A double decker Express bus Line A (plain). For Terminal B double decker Express bus Line B (plain).

● To Piraeus. Piraeus yellow express bus 19 every 15 mins between 0600 and midnight (and every half hour from midnight to 0600), calling at the West Airport on the way. Also blue bus 101 to Klissovis/Theotaki.

**Athens Airport (West)** This is smaller than the East terminal, although extension work is in progress. Departures are on the right, and arrivals on the left, each with its domestic and international section. Many buses stop in the rather cramped forecourt, including:

● To the city centre. Double decker Express bus A or B (red diagonal stripe) to Syntagma and Omonia. Olympic Airways bus every 30 mins to Syntagma (100 drs). Blue bus 133 every half hour to Syntagma, also blue bus 122 every 20 mins to Vassilisis Olgas.

● To the mainline railway stations. Double decker Express bus Line B (red diagonal stripe) or via City Centre and change.

● To the long distance bus terminals. For Terminal A double decker Express bus Line A (red diagonal stripe). For Terminal B double decker Express bus Line B (red diagonal stripe).

● To Piraeus. Piraeus yellow express bus 19 on its way from the East Airport (see above for timing). Also blue bus 109 every 20 mins to Klissovis/Theotaki.

FIVE

# Accommodation

## Hotels

Greek hotels are strictly classified and supervised by the NTOG, in conjunction with the tourist police. The top grade, Luxury, is the only one unrestricted by any price control. Next come hotels graded A to E — although these gradings must be rather flexibly interpreted. This is decided by the quality and amount of facilities available — something like a room telephone can upgrade it from C to B. Standards also vary from island to island; but to put it in proportion, a difference of one grade may only mean paying another £1 per night. The best rooms of the more popular hotels are often contracted to package operators. Some hotels offer 'bungalow' accommodation, sometimes self-catering, grouped around central facilities. Conventional baths are rare in Greece, except in top grade hotels, and showers are the norm. Water heating is usually by solar panel, so showers are hotter in the evening. Towels and soap are normally provided.

## Pensions

These are small purpose-built blocks of accommodation, usually with ensuite toilet and shower, and offered on a bed and breakfast basis (the breakfast is normally taken at a nearby taverna). They offer cheaper and more flexible accommodation than hotels.

## Service flats

These are blocks of accommodation suitable for self-catering. Standards of construction and finish are rather variable. The tourist agencies, usually positioned to intercept the tourist as he stumbles off the boat, will have the details.

## Private accommodation

Privately owned houses are often available for rent, which can give very good value for groups or families travelling together. Facilities will naturally include a kitchen. Village rooms, on the other hand, are simply for sleeping in. They are often within the house of a Greek family, although increasingly they are being purpose-built, sometimes with en suite shower and toilet. Prices are controlled, and each room should contain a notice giving details. A room grade A is equivalent to a hotel room grade C, private grade B to hotel grade D, and private grade C to hotel grade E. The owner may be prepared to take less, out of season. Meals, if any, would be by private arrangement.

Increasingly the tourist agencies are handling the business of private lettings, which is probably just as well. But often women with free rooms will come down to meet the ferries, or accost tourists in the streets, even though the practice is supposed to be illegal. Many a village quarrel has been caused by the 'poaching' of tourists, who were thought to have committed themselves to another. Complaints, if necessary, and initial enquiries too, can always be made to the police.

## Camping

Although the NTOG itself runs a number of campsites on the mainland, with reliable standards and reasonable services, it has none on the islands. Indeed there are fewer campsites on the islands, in relation to demand, than on the mainland; during the season their capacity is severely stretched. An island with several campsites gives no better chance of finding a place, but only shows that the island is attractive to campers. NTOG is doing what it can to encourage the opening of more sites, but progress is slow. A particular difficulty seems to be the rather high specifications insisted on for new sites, which involve a capital outlay beyond the means of many islanders. On other islands the authorities do not wish to encourage campers, because of the poor image acquired by too many of that fraternity. Unofficial campsites, which open adventitiously during the season, can sometimes be found in olive groves, fields, or patches of land next to hotels and restaurants. Fees are likely to be about half those for licensed sites, but for fewer facilities. Particulars of functioning official campsites are listed under each island in Parts 2 and 3 (limited in this volume to Thassos, Samothraki, Skiathos and Skiros). This camping section also discusses the scope for free camping, the water situation, and availability of Camping Gas exchange bottles (expendable cartridges are widely stocked).

Camping outside campsites is supposed to be illegal in Greece, and notices to this effect are frequently seen. But large numbers of holidaymakers do arrive, either expecting to be able to camp, or prepared to do so in the event of cheap lodgings not being readily available. Police attitudes vary from island to island; but in general it would be contrary to Greek traditions of hospitality, besides damaging for the tourist trade, to turn campers away. In any case the small numbers of police are greatly overstretched during the season. Usually they confine themselves to going through the motions of moving campers on, from time to time: these token gestures become more vigorous only in response to complaints (about noise, smell or other nuisance) from local residents or resentful owners of hotels and campsites.

Otherwise the main preoccupation of the authorities is the fearful danger of forest fires, which can so easily be started by careless campers. Every summer television news programmes show scenes of forest fires raging out of control, in spite of the efforts of fire brigades supported by relays of seaplanes, drenching the blaze with tons of seawater to contain them. The ferocity and terror of these infernoes has to be experienced to be believed, whilst the dismal and totally wasteful consequences are to be seen in parts of most islands. Campers and people who smoke should bear this in mind at all times. Article 206 of Law 86/69 can be rigorously applied, stating as it does that 'The punishment for lighting a fire in the forest, *for whatever purpose*, is at least two months in prison' . This is one Greek law which it would be unwise to trifle with. (Drug smuggling would come into the same category)

SIX

# Food, drink and entertainment

## What to expect of Greek food

Few people would place Greek cooking very high in a league table of *haute cuisine*. And it is undeniable that general standards on the islands fall below those on the mainland. Further, the choice is more limited. At its best, Greek island food is fresh, tasty and satisfying. The problem is that during the summer, because kitchens are unbearably hot, and probably large numbers of hungry customers sit waiting to be served, standards fall below their best. Naturally these are generalisations, to which there are exceptions.

Many islanders themselves enjoy eating out, but not usually in those establishments along the waterfront and other places frequented by large numbers of tourists. Tucked away inside the town or out in the countryside are little places where they can enjoy traditional meals in a customary atmosphere. It's normal for these meals to be served warm, rather than hot — that's the way they prefer it!

International cooking, sometimes done very well, is found in some big hotels and a few restaurants in the more sophisticated islands. Most larger restaurants offer some choice of international dishes, in addition to Greek food. Smaller restaurants tend to specialise in fish *(psaria)* or meat *(skaras)* - both usually served grilled. Fish nowadays tends to be rather expensive, but looks even more so on menus, when the written price usually indicates price per kilo — so a single portion will cost only a fraction of that. At the lowest end of the scale comes the humble *taverna,* comparable to the French *bistro* and Italian *trattoria* — a place where simple cooking can be enjoyed amid modest surroundings. The main difference between taverna and restaurant is that the latter opens at lunchtime as well as in the evening and probably provides a small selection of desserts, coffee and after dinner drinks. But thanks to some well known films, and abetted by tourist propaganda, the taverna image has been overlain with notions of music, dancing and mingling with the locals, in some romantic situation beside a starlit beach. Tourists therefore come to the islands eager to eat in tavernas. And so many restaurants have found it necessary to describe themselves as tavernas!

The Greeks are great nibblers of food in between meals, if need be straight out of some plastic packet. But long before Colonel Sanders made his mark on the West, they already had years of experience of convenience food. Most island towns have at least one *souvlaki* stall, probably opening in the late morning as well as the evening — even if in the more sophisticated islands you find it disguised as a snack bar. The proper filling of the *souvlaki* is some chunks of grilled lamb, mixed with raw tomato, onion and spices, wrapped in a small pancake called *pitta*. Unfortunately rather ordinary bread rolls are often substituted for *pitta* and, what is more, sometimes not even toasted as they should be. A number on the price list 1, 2 or 3 indicates the number of skewers of meat

*This Thassian beekeeper inspects the occupants of one of his many hives, spread out along a bank beside the road. Neither he nor the small boy helping him — who did not want to be photographed — wear any protective clothing. On Thassos local honey is good and cheap, and on sale everywhere.*

included in the filling. Many variations on the souvlaki, including close approximations to hamburgers and hot dogs, can be found. Other popular convenience snacks include cheese pies *(tiropites)* and toasted sandwiches *(tost)*. Increasingly too pizzerias are found, their product more in the French rather than Italian style.

Many establishments use a standardised menu, with a vast range of dishes printed on it. In fact only those with prices beside them are available (the two prices are with and without tax). In any case it's quite the done thing to go into the kitchen to see precisely what is on offer. It's usual to leave a 10 per cent tip, divided between the waiter and the boy who brought the bread and drinks. Restaurants sometimes have two price lists, the cheaper one being for dishes taken away. Whole sheep or goats, roasted on the spit, are sometimes sold in take-away portions, costed by weight.

Much nibbling also goes on in cafés (more correctly *kafeneions*). These are primarily in the business of serving drinks of all kinds: hot and cold, beers, wines and spirits. But so long do the Greeks have to wait for their evening meal that it is normal, even prudent, to nibble something with the aperitif. This is called *mezes* (sing) or *mezethes* (plural), and in the more traditional drinking places is probably included in the price of the drink: otherwise it can be ordered and paid for separately.

Two other typically Greek types of eating place are the *galaklopoleio,* specialising in milk products and sometimes honey, and the *zacharoplasteion,* which specialises in cakes and pastries. The former can be useful at breakfast, as an alternative to a taverna, whilst the latter is fine for a mid morning or afternoon snack, as well as the best place to come for your sweet course, after an evening meal at a taverna.

Greek coffee is similar to Turkish — but better not order it as such! It is always served black in a *demi-tasse* with an accompanying glass of cold water. Never stir it, and beware of the considerable amount of sediment at the bottom. You choose your amount of sugar: without *skéto*; with a little sugar *médrio*; incredibly sweet *gleekó*.

# Drinks

Greek beer is good, another legacy from King Otto, who brought techniques, equipment and a skilled *braumeister* down from his native Bavaria. The oldest and best known brand has been *Fix,* but *Amstel* and *Henninger* are more often found in the bars today. Cheap Greek wines may prove rather disappointing, compared with a French *vin du pays* or Italian *vino di tavola:* too often they are mass produced or, if local, have been crudely made. Most of the medium and dry white wines are at least slightly resinated. The Greeks prefer it that way — the habit is no more debased than smoking menthol cigarettes, however the purist may dislike it! As for the famous and controversial *retsina,* that is best thought of as in a class of its own.

Red wines are not often resinated, but instead may well seem rather sweet to a foreign palate. A bottle with *demi-doux* on the label will probably be very sweet indeed. The few dryer red wines, on the other hand, are often quite pleasant. Also agreeable, especially for drinking late into the evening, are some sweet white wines, such as the celebrated wine of Samos which was a favourite with Lord Byron.

The native Greek spirits are brandy and ouzo. Both seem amazingly cheap, especially when bought direct from the barrel into your own empty bottle. Cheap brandy, though undeniably potent, may disappoint on account of its crude, sweet, perfumed and almost soapy flavour. Better qualities come mostly in the bottle, graded from three to seven stars — the higher the number the more mature (and expensive, of course). *Cambas* and *Metaxas* are reliable brands, found everywhere. The cheaper ouzo, on the other hand, often seems very good, especially when made locally. Ouzo is an aniseed flavoured spirit, colourless when neat, which turns milky when water is added. Thus it is a close relative of *pastis* and similar drinks found throughout the Mediterranean. When served in a café, a large glass of water will invariably accompany it. They do not need to be drunk mixed. But if retribution by hangover is to be avoided, by one means or another a lot of water must be drunk.

There are several types of traditional Greek drinking place, from *kafeneion,* through *kafebar,* to *ouzerie.* It's very rare indeed to find a Greek woman in any of these, although foreign girls will be tolerated. But foreigners of both sexes may find the atmosphere too rigid and male-dominated to be congenial, and prefer instead the warmer ambience of a pub. Prices will be significantly higher because these places do little business outside the tourist season; but the owner — an educated Greek or expatriate — will be prepared to chat to you for hours, dispensing all the free local information you could ask for, in an atmosphere of soft lights and taped music.

Drink (and food) price levels are all authorised by the tourist police, who take into account the facilities available before setting the prices. Thus the same beer bought for 50 drs in a café, may cost 100drs in a pub or 150 drs at a discothque. The cheapest way to get round high drink prices is to buy a bottle of wine and share it.

*Old men drinking ouzo. Many elderly men proudly wear their traditional costume as a matter of course. Prices are cheap in this little café which, unusually, displays a drinks list perfectly understandable by most foreign tourists.*

## Entertainment

Nightclubs are found in the larger island capitals, in the big hotels, and occasionally elsewhere.

Most towns have a cinema, where the soundtrack is normally in the original language, with subtitles in Greek. There are additional open-air cinemas in summer. The demand from younger holidaymakers ensures that discos of some sort are found on all the main islands. They are usually situated on the outskirts of towns and villages and ownership and even location are prone to change from year to year, so these are not specifically listed in Parts 2 and 3. Not all discos make an admission charge, but where they do it will include the price of your first drink.

Traditional *bouzouki* can be heard on most islands, sometimes played by live musicians in a restaurant or special club. The dancing that often spontaneously accompanies it is known as *syrtaki* (though there are other forms of dance); non-Greek onlookers may well be encouraged to join in as the evening wears on!

On the radio there are daily news programmes and weather forecasts in English. On weekdays there is also a daily news bulletin on television. This follows the 1800 evening news in Greek, on the Second Programme, and usually finishes with a brief weather forecast.

## Sport and recreation

Caiques can sometimes be hired by the day or hour, for **fishing** or private excursions. Otherwise it should be possible to make arrangements to accompany a fishing caique. Pedalos, often for hire on the more popular beaches, can be made use of for limited fishing excursions.

Caique owners should be able to suggest favourable spots to find fish. They may even supply the gear. Alternatively some specialist shops do exist where fishing tackle can be bought or hired. Greek fishermen usually dig their own bait from some sandy beach; but maggots are sometimes sold.

Fish are less plentiful than they used to be, and now that Greece has joined the EEC Italian boats often come across in pursuit of the choicer species. But out in open waters where the *meltemi* cools the surface water, the vertical convection currents thus created increase the amount of plankton available to support the fish population.

Breathing apparatus can sometimes be hired for underwater **swimming.** Its use is restricted by law to designated areas, in order to prevent the plundering of antiquities, and only hand-operated spears should be used.

There are few public **tennis** courts in Greece, but those belonging to the big hotels are often available for hire to non-residents, together with equipment. There is a **golf** course on Skiathos. Donkeys, mules or horses can sometimes be hired for **riding** excursions. **Bicycles** can usually be hired in tourist areas. Details are given in Parts 2 and 3.

*A communal water tap. Most of the North Aegean islands are well watered, so communal taps and fountains are found in practically all the villages.*

SEVEN

# Shopping

The cost of living on an island — any island — is almost bound to be greater than on the mainland, since the great majority of goods consumed (and virtually all the tourist goods) are nowadays brought in from outside, and so must bear the quite considerable cost of sea transport. In Lemnos, for example, this adds some 6 drachmae per kilo to the wholesale cost of everything imported. On the other hand North Aegean islands are supplied from the North Greek mainland, where prices are considerably cheaper than further south: so their prices are perhaps comparable to those in similar sized towns and villages in the Athens area.

The transport factor may occasionally work to the tourist's advantage, if an island's own products are exported in quantity. Thus honey in Thassos, and sponges in Lemnos, cost less than on the mainland. Fruit and vegetables seesaw between scracity and abundance. Sometimes lorries arrive from the mainland, piled high with surplus from the markets that must be sold very quickly; at such times remarkable bargains can be had. But at other times prices seem high in relation to their unremarkable quality, which rarely compares with Italy or the South of France. Choice is also limited — lettuce for example, can be hard to find.

Greek produced goods in general seem quite reasonably priced, whilst imports of all sorts are more expensive. Cigarettes are an example, with local brands costing but a fraction of imports. The tobacco, mostly grown in the north of the country, is usually good, but tightness of packing and effectiveness of the filter may seem inferior. A degree of bargaining over the more expensive tourist goods is usually in order. Ceramics, leather, cheesecloth dresses, silver jewellery, sponges and worry beads *(komboloi)* are usually good value. Camera film is rather expensive, and may also have deteriorated with the heat.

There are few things that cost sufficiently more in Greece to make it worth bringing them out from home. Photographic film may be an exception, whilst black and white film is impossible to find on many islands. If you plan to be self-catering, beef stock cubes, coffee whitener and bran fibre are about the only things of any consequence you'll probably not find in an island supermarket.

## Shop opening hours

These are controlled by law. Food shops, for example, are supposed to stay closed for three evenings of the week as well as all day on Sunday, regulations that are observed in traditional places. But in holiday areas they are not; of course there is a period of closing in the middle of the day but after that shops stay open as long as the owner thinks there is a chance of doing business.

Street kiosks *(periptero)* also open for an amazingly long period, often without lunch break. They sell a wide range of small items, most obviously books and magazines, postcards and cigarettes. Some of them also keep a telephone with meter for public use (see below).

## Books and newspapers

Most islands have shops where English language books can be bought. This usually takes the form of a display rack containing a standard selection of popular paperbacks. Where there are lots of tourists the choice improves. Prices are at least 50% above UK prices.

The more popular tourist islands have shops where used foreign language books can be exchanged. You choose between paying a small fee per book exchanged, or taking away half the number of books brought in, without payment.

UK daily and Sunday papers arrive regularly in the tourist islands, sometimes as soon as the day after printing, depending on distance from Athens. A locally produced alternative is the Athens News.

## Currency and banks

Greek currency is denominated in drachmae. At the time of writing (1988) the rate of exchange in the UK was approaching 250 drs = £1 sterling, although the tourist in Greece would get a less favourable rate. Thus each drachma is worth less than ½p. In theory the drachma divides into 100 lepta. Notes of 1000, 500, 100 and 50 drachmae, and coins of 50, 20, 10, 5, and 1 are in common use. A new 5000 note has been introduced, but is often difficult to get changed. The old ½ drachma coin is no longer legal tender, whilst the 50dr note is on the way out. Small change is sometimes in short supply.

There is no limit to the amount of foreign currency permitted to be brought into Greece. Nor, if it was properly declared on entry, is the proportion that can be taken out again restricted. But the amount of local currency permitted to be brought in or out is closely controlled, but has recently been increased from 3000drs to an altogether more practical 25,000drs per person .

The main islands have branches of national banks — usually the National Bank of Greece and the Commercial Bank of Greece. These can handle any transaction in which the tourist might be interested. The minor islands have banking facilities, usually organised by a travel agent or prominent shopkeeper, in association with one of the national banks. Foreign currency and travellers cheques, including Eurocheques denominated in drachmae can probably be changed, although the rate of exchange may well be determined by reference to the local newspaper. Cheques drawn on the UK National Giro can be changed for drachmae at any Greek post office.

Standard banking hours are from about 8am to 2pm Mondays to Fridays. During the season some banks in island capitals may open for a couple of hours later in the afternoon. Saturday opening can be encountered in Athens and other large towns on the mainland. Banks at road frontiers and Athens airport are also open on Sundays. Outside banking hours the larger hotels often change money, even for non-residents — but naturally at a less favourable rate. On Monday mornings long queues of newly arrived tourists usually form outside the banks.

If you plan to stay longer than three months in Greece, save the pink exchange slips, as you will need them when applying for a visa.

## Post offices

**Poste restante** mail seems to be scrupulously handled by island post offices (*taxydromeion,* the x pronounced as h). It will be held for at least the statutory four weeks, for collection against identification (passport), before eventually being returned to sender. Naturally, some difficulties can occur over deciphering handwriting in the Latin alphabet. Whilst letters are filed alphabetically, they may well be found under a forename or title, even Mr. Mrs or Esq. Most officials will cooperate if politely asked to have another look.

**Postage stamps** are on sale in post offices. But it may be more convenient to use a shop or kiosk — mostly stamps are kept wherever postcards are sold. Such establishments are legally entitled to charge 10% over and above the face value of the stamps.

## Telephones

Telephone kiosks have either blue or orange bands at the top of their sides. The blue ones are for domestic calls, and use 10dr coins. Only the relatively few kiosks with an orange box can be used for international calls; these take 10, 20 and 50dr coins. All these boxes are prone to faults — though rarely through vandalism — and you can get cut off if you fail to spot the tiny dim red light that's supposed to give warning. Thus it's often simpler to use the metered phone in an hotel, restaurant or *periptero*. In addition each town has an OTE (pronounced oh tay) office with booths containing metered telephones. The counter clerk will allocate you a booth and take your money on completion. In any case, OTE prices are cheaper than elsewhere. Telegrams are also handled, but it's cheaper to phone.

The international prefix for the UK from Greece is 0044, followed by the UK STD code, less any initial 0.

EIGHT

# Your health and comfort

## Medical care

Doctors and chemists entirely adequate to the needs of tourism are found in all the main islands. Moreover in the area of the Saronic Gulf transport to Athens or Corinth is very easily arranged. Doctors come regularly to all the villages to hold surgeries. The buildings concerned are usually central and self-evident, with a notice giving the hours of attendance. They are often staffed by young 'barefoot doctors', doing their initial post-qualification period. Unless this is served in a rural area, salaries paid to these young doctors are very low indeed.

In theory, possession of form E. 111 (see DHSS leaflet SA 30) entitles you to medical treatment at token cost. That should even include transportation costs to a mainland hospital if necessary. (Military helicopters are often used in emergency from remote islands, occasionally even a passing submarine has been pressed into service.) In practice, for reasons that include the impossibility of completing the required paperwork on some islands, holidaymakers may well have to settle for private treatment. So it would be foolish to come out without insurance cover. But the cost of private consultations and prescriptions is less than in northern Europe — currently a consultation costs about 1, 000drs.

No vaccination certificates are required for entry into Greece from the UK, but the DHSS recommend protection against typhoid. A booster injection is needed every three years.

## Burns and bites

Care needs to be taken when starting sunbathing, because cooling winds can disguise the real heat of the sun — half an hour's exposure may well be enough for the first time. Mosquitoes can be a great hazard on most of the islands, as they are throughout much of the Mediterranean. Some hotels and campsites carry out successful preventative programmes in their own vicinities, but the extent of the nuisance is impossible to predict. Fortunately products to kill or repell mosquitoes and to sooth stings can be bought virtually everywhere — as also can creams and lotions for use before and after sunbathing — and these are usually cheaper than at home.

## Water

Town drinking water is normally bacteriologically safe, but may well be strongly mineralised. Good bottled drinking waters are widely and cheaply available. Comments on the water supply situation on each island are found in Parts 2 and 3 under the camping section.

## Toilets

Public conveniences are seen much less often than at home; the vicinity of any bus station or food market can be fruitful. Whilst local people are liable on occasion to take advantage of the nearest bush, it is normally acceptable to make use of facilities in a hotel or bar. It is not even necessary to be a customer, but they prefer it when you are!. Ask for the *toe alletta*.

Toilets are usually of the 'hole in the ground' type; the knack of using them is soon acquired, and they are easier to keep clean with a hose-pipe. Be careful not to lose the contents of your pocket down the hole! The fastidious should bring their own toilet paper, just in case. You might also like to be prepared, with one of those 'universal' type of basin plugs in your pocket.

## Electricity

The 220v AC supply, compatible with UK domestic appliances, is now almost universal in Greece. Power sockets are usually for plugs of the German type — two pins with double earthing strap. Double-earthed travel appliances can safely be connected via a continental two pin adaptor. Light bulbs use screw type sockets.

*A farmer leads his donkey to market along the beach below Rupert Brooke's statue, Skiros (see page 183).*

NINE

# About the North Aegean islands

## Agriculture

The climate of the Aegean is not particularly favourable for agriculture. In winter the land lies heavy, wet, cold and windswept: in summer it bakes beneath a blazing sun. Amounts of level fertile land are rather small on most of the islands. The mountains are, at best, suitable only for timber; otherwise the remaining parts are generally rough, stony and sloping. Arable crops can be grown there only after laborious terracing.

Grain continues to be grown on the best land, as well as some market garden crops where transport to wholesale markets is easy. Otherwise fruit and vegetables are grown only on a small scale. Less fertile land unsuitable for mechanical operations has often been abandoned for arable crops, though it may still serve for fodder or grazing. Marginal land is used for those two great mainstays of Mediterranean agriculture, olives and grapes. Once established, both crops continue to produce without much further expense (whereas grubbing and clearing the land would call for fresh investment). But both are now in oversupply. The EEC has mountains of butter competing with oil for culinary use, and lakes of surplus wine. And although both oil and wine are ideal for trading, occupying but a small volume in relation to value, prices are currently very low; whereas the 'terms of trade' against imported motor cars, household appliances and high technology generally are unfavourable.

It was not always so. In classical times the joys of wine were as much appreciated as today, and chieftains expected to provide it for their loyal followers. Olives were even more valuable then than now, providing an important element in diet, a substitute for soap, and the sole easily available fuel for lamps. Skilful husbandry would produce surplus oil and wine for export, so much grain and other useful commodities could be got in return.

That was one of the factors making it possible in ancient times for small islands to support much larger populations than they can today. But as knowledge of production techniques spread into Italy and Asia Minor, the commercial advantage was lost. From then on populations could only diminish, and the trading advantage of the islands fall away.

## Beaches

Most of the islands are well endowed with beaches, and the more popular ones are discussed in Parts 2 and 3. Most of these enjoy at least the services of a drinks seller during the season, whilst many have a taverna near at hand. Waterskiing, windsurfing, sailing and boating are often to be found at the popular beaches: some sort of instruction is usually available.

Greek law officially forbids nudity, which most Greek island people find genuinely offensive. Where callous individuals peel off completely on their town beaches, mothers feel obliged to take an alternative route home with their school children. To prevent such public nuisance, police have been known to don swimming trunks and look for naturists, before returning in uniform to make their arrests. In fact those islands frequented by foreign tourists normally have at least one isolated beach set aside where nudism/naturism is unofficially tolerated. As for toplessness, it is nowadays more or less acceptable on any isolated beach: the higher the proportion of foreigners to Greeks, the more it is seen.

Sandy beaches seem preferred by most holidaymakers. But rocky beaches have their advantages too, especially for snorkelling in the clearer water. Those without flippers would be wise to wear plastic beach-shoes; rocks can become very slippery, whilst prickly sea-urchins may lie concealed below. There is a law restricting the use of underwater breathing apparatus - both for swimming and fishing - to certain designated areas, which was introduced to prevent plundering of underwater antiquities by would-be treasure hunters. (See also page 119). In practice nobody is likely to be prevented from using this gear around tourist beaches.

Jelly fish seem to be on the increase everywhere these days. Travelling around in small shoals, they come and go unpredictably since, though chiefly driven by wind and current, they can also propel themselves. They come in a wide range of sizes and colours, the transparent ones being most difficult to spot, whilst the pale brown ones have the worst sting. This is certainly painful for a few hours, but an anti-allergic jelly, as used for insect bites, may help. Ammonia is another panacea, available in a sachet at the pharmacy; even closer to hand, it's readily available in the form of urine!

It is traditional Greek custom to take the first bathe of the year on Ascension Day, which falls 40 days after Easter. But for us northerners the sea should not seem too cold even at Easter.

## Road systems

Not so many years have passed since all island roads were mule tracks, once kept to a very high state of repair, as can be seen today on the Mount Athos peninsula, and short sections in good order are still found on some islands. But with their declining economic importance many have become rough, although often still in regular use. Except for Alonissos and Agios Efstratios, all the islands now have a basic network of tarmac road. This is wide enough for the bus, and certainly presents no difficulty for private motor cars. The extent of this network is shown on each map, although additions continue to be made. There are also a number of unsurfaced motor tracks, often recently bulldozed, and wide enough for lorry traffic. Some of these are an essential part of the island road network, and await only the funds to permit a layer of tarmac. Then there are tracks to meet the needs of forestry and forest recreation, others whose primary purpose is agriculture, and yet others supporting mining and quarrying. The condition of these varies widely, depending on recent weather, terrain, and the time elapsed since they were last graded. Private cars can often travel considerable distances on these tracks, without too much discomfort. But sometimes at critical points they become impassable.

It is certainly true that the holidaymaker can manage quite well without his own car especially on the smaller islands. All (except Agios Efstratios) have at least one taxi, most many more. All (except Agios Efstratios) have a bus service. Bicycles and motorbikes, and sometimes motorcars, can be hired. But if a car has already been brought to Greece, it will probably be convenient to continue to have the use of it.

Petrol and diesel fuel can be obtained on all the islands (except Agios Efstratios), and the number of stations is adequate in relation to the road network. Proficient repair of routine defects can be made on the more important islands.

## Motorbike and moped rental

Motorbikes, or more usually mopeds, are readily available on most of the islands, and many of us will tempted to hire one, regardless of our riding experience. Most hire bikes have seen better days, and signs of rough treatment can usually be hidden under a coat of paint. Some important points to remember when hiring are:

● Make sure it works. Take it for a test run, which will also ensure you can handle it!

● Negotiate the price, especially if hiring for more than a day. Does this include petrol? What insurance cover is included?

● Make a note of the agency 'phone number in case of breakdown. They have their own breakdown trucks and don't sit idle for long!

● Don't be ashamed to ask for a crash helmet. They are not compulsory in Greece, and they won't do a thing to enhance your sporting image. But they cost no extra, and may prove to be your salvation: there are so many "holiday drivers" around in summer that even if *you* know what you are doing, you may fall foul of someone else who doesn't. Accidents happen every day. Most people get away with cuts and bruises: but whenever you see that helicopter passing overhead, someone has been badly injured and is on his way to hospital.

● Make a firm arrangement about the time you will return the bike. Your hire may be "for the day", but if you return it after 1900 you'll find yourself unpopular with the employee who has had to work late for you. If you want to keep it until first thing next morning, make that clear.

● Don't forget they drive on the right hand side in Greece!

● When roads are poor, look for a bike with large wheels. If you want to go up into the mountains, try for a more powerful motor.

● Resist the temptation to take corners at speed.

If the engine stops functioning, check first that there is still petrol (*vin zeé nee*) in the tank. Otherwise the problem probably lies with the ignition. Is the cable firmly attached to the sparking plug? Or indeed, is the sparking plug still in place?

Remember it is against the law to drive motorised bikes through towns during the siesta (i.e. from 1300 to 1700), or indeed to make other loud noises.

# Maps and walking excursions

Locally produced maps can be bought on most islands. These are useful for making excursions, despite the quite substantial errors they usually contain. New developments are often incorrectly incorporated, whilst tracks that disappeared years ago may still be retained.

Suggestions for walking excursions are given for each island. Where mule tracks are involved a stout pair of walking shoes is advisable. Where a time is given, this is for the single journey, by an averagely fit adult walking steadily. There would be wide differences for an experienced hiker, or a family party.

*The olive crop becomes ready for harvest during the autumn. It is dislodged from the branches by beating vigorously with a long cane. Nets may be used to help gather up the fallen fruit, but otherwise much hand labour is needed for retrieval.*
*Traditionally, the whole family participates in olive gathering.*

# Time and distance

It's not wise to rely too closely on any estimates you may be given for time or distance. Local people do not think of journeys in simple terms of kilometers or minutes; in any case, for reasons of courtesy, they hold it more important to please you with optimism rather than disappoint you with inconvenient reality. For similar reasons commercial signposts often understate distances to campsites and other attractions — sometimes even an official signpost errs.

Beware too that *p. m.* in Greek, *prin mesimeri,* is before noon; *m.m., meta mesimeri,* is after noon.

Summer time in Greece is now fully co-ordinated with most other European countries: thus Greek local time is two hours ahead of time in the UK, so long as the dates for British Summer Time keep in step with Europe.

# Highlights of history affecting the North Agean Islands

### Prehistoric times

**6500 BC** Approximate date when the first farmer settlers crossed the Bosphorus to arrive in Europe. There is plenty of fertile land for all comers, with no need for fortifications or weapons. Primitive boats already existed, so probably before long some settlers cross to the nearer and more fertile islands.

**2800 BC** End of the Neolithic Age. Beginning of the Bronze Age.

**2600 BC** Beginning of the Minoan civilisation in Crete, where the skills of metalwork and pottery develop to great heights. Much trade, especially with Egypt. A time of great prosperity, with Minoan fleets keeping the peace of the Aegean.

**1950 BC** Arrival and spread of the first Greek-speaking Indo-Europeans on the mainland.

**1450 BC** Minoan civilisation falls, because of disruptions to trade, raiders from outside, and natural disasters. At about the same time a Greek-speaking kingdom based on Mycenae begins to dominate the mainland, then the Aegean and beyond. Mycenaean ships ply the seas as pirates and traders.

**1183 BC** Traditional, and possibly accurate date for the fall of Troy. The cause of that long war, according to Homer, is the abduction by Trojan Paris of the beautiful Helen, wife of Mycenaean chieftain Menelaus. In reality it is probably more to do with trading restrictions, preventing access to profitable opportunities beyond the Dardanelles.

**1100 BC** Beginning of the Iron Age. Ownership of effective arms has hitherto been limited to the few who could afford bronze. Now cheap weapons can be had by all. The Dorians, last Greek-speaking tribe to reach Greece, may already have mastered smelting techniques before their arrival. Aristocratic Mycenae, weakened by over-indulgence in warfare, is now dealt the final blow. Athens, perhaps alone among established cities, holds out against the Dorians.

### The Hellonistic City-State

Refugees from the Dorians found new cities in Asia Minor, where the standards of Greek civilisation are kept alive during the 'Dark Ages'. Phoenician seamen take over the trading function of Mycenae.

**C 800 BC** Homer, possibly a native of Chios, puts into writing the Iliad and Odyssey. Old tales of gods and heroes in Mycenaean times are definitively recorded.

**766 BC** The first Olympic Games contest.

**700-500 BC** The Archaic Period. A great flowering of city states. Experiments with political systems evolve into the essentials of Greek civilisation. As land becomes insufficient for the increasing population, a wave of colonisation sweeps out into Italy (Magna Graecia), then into the Aegean and Asia Minor. Power polarises between Athens and Sparta.

Themistokles, anticipating invasion from Persia, persuades the Athenian assembly to invest the profits from silver mines newly discovered at Laurion (Lavrion) in a fleet of 200 triremes.

**500-478 BC** The Persian Wars. Greek and Persian expansionisms interlock in conflict. The first invasion, ordered by Darius, is turned back at the battle of Marathon. His successor Xerxes himself leads the subsequent invasion, unexpectedly repulsed at the naval battle of Salamis (480).

**478-431 BC** The great age of Hellenism. Triumphant Athens assumes leadership in all things. Persians expelled from the Aegean, and piracy cleaned up again. Athens gradually loses popularity, because of its excessive power, ambition, and collection of stiff financial 'contributions' from unwilling allies. The final straw comes when Athens expropriates the League Treasury from reasonably neutral Delos, to hold it in Athens itself.

**431-404 BC** The Peloponnesian War. Sparta takes the lead to topple Athens. A disastrous defeat in far off Syracuse marks the beginning of the end for Athens.

Subsequent struggles between Sparta and its former allies weaken them all.

### The Hellenistic Age

**359-336 BC** Rise of Macedon, under Philip II until his murder.

**336-323 BC** Alexander the Great unleashes the power accumulated under his father. His empire covers vast areas of Asia and North Africa. After his death it immediately begins to crumble. But fertilisation by Hellenic culture of the older Eastern civilisation is of lasting influence.

**323-200 BC** Most of Greece retrogresses into the role of a neglected and oppressed province of Macedon.

**202 BC** The defeat of Carthage by Rome.

### The Graeco-Roman Period

Roman incursions into Greece eventually culminate in the Sack of Corinth (146 BC) and incorporation as a province of the Roman Empire. Julius Caesar himself when young was captured and ransomed by pirates. Under Pompey Rome once again cleanses the Aegean of pirates (67 BC).

**295 AD** Finding his empire too large, and with too many problems to be ruled by one man from a single centre, Diocletian divides it into Western and Eastern parts.

### Early Christian and Byzantine Age

The first Christian emperor, Constantine (died 337 BC), builds a defensible capital for his Eastern Empire on the site of the former Greek Byzantium.

**381 AD** The Second Ecumenical Council grants the Bishop of Constantinople jurisdiction over the Church in Asia Minor and the Balkans. The future Greek Orthodox Church is thus legitimised.

(**Opposite**) *A climb up from Skiros town to the Acropolis gives superb views over serried ranks of flat-topped roofs and the valley beyond. In the foreground is part of the Monastery of St. George.*

Athens sinks to the level of a minor provincial city, whereas Salonica (Thessaloniki) becomes second city of the Empire.

**393 AD** The Olympic Games are suppressed, nudity now being offensive to Christian Byzantines.

Over the centuries Byzantium deals with invasions by Goths, Huns, Vandals, Slavs, Arabs and Bulgars, with varying success.

**1042-1071** Norman adventurers seize Byzantine territories in Italy, and go on to found a kingdom in Sicily. Byzantium attempts to repel the Norman threat with help from Venice, granting over-generous trading rights in return.

**1096** Start of the First Crusade, which turns out unexpectedly successful. Knights from Western Europe, mainly French, fight against the Saracens in the Holy Land. Afterwards some find themselves rulers of petty kingdoms in the Near East. The beginning of the 'Frankish Territories' (the Byzantines call all Latin-speaking Christians Franks).

**1155** Byzantium grants trade concessions to the Genoese, in an attempt to counterbalance the Venetian advantage.

### Franks, Venetians and Turks

**1204** The disgraceful capture of Christian Constantinople by Christian Crusaders is masterminded by Venice for commercial advantage (and in revenge for a recent massacre of Venetian merchants in Constantinople). Much of the Greek mainland and many islands become, for a time, Frankish territories. Their rulers, few in number, and fully preoccupied with defence of their borders, gladly accept Venetian and Genoese offers to lease island ports for trading posts. After some time Italians become effective rulers of many of these islands.

**1261** A final flowering of the arts takes place under the Palaeologos dynasty, whilst the empire withers.

**1453** Fall of Constantinople to the Ottoman Turks. The Mount Athos monastic state is left on its own to uphold the Greek Orthodox religion.

As the Ottoman empire expands, Aegean islands become progressively Turkish.

**1683** Turkish expansion culminates in the Siege of Vienna.

**(Opposite)** *A religious procession winds its way up the narrow streets of Skiros, towards the Monastery of St. George.*

**1699** In an astonishing reversal, the Turks are forced to surrender all Hungary to the Austrians. Turkey begins to become the 'Sick man of Europe'.

**1715** In a final spasm, the Turks remove Venice from Crete, its last Aegean possession.

**1770-1774** Catherine the Great leads Russia into expansionary adventures, with a fleet in the Aegean. Her aim is to destroy the Ottoman empire, and set up instead a client Greek state straddling the Bosphorus. The alarm of European Great Powers limits her success. But the right of Russian ships to pass at will through what has been a closed Ottoman lake is recognised. And since at that time the Russians have few ships of their own, Greek shipowners can be licensed to fly the Russian flag, leading to the rise of Greek shipowning magnates on suitably remote islands (such as Hydra, Spetses and Psara). Before long Aegean-Black Sea trade becomes effectively a Greek monopoly.

As Turkish power weakens, ideas of freedom ferment in the Balkans. At the same time satellite Ottoman rulers become too powerful to be controlled from Constantinople.

**1810** Local patriots combine forces with brigands and outlaws to start the Greek revolution.

**1811** Mehemet Ali emerges as master of Egypt. After consolidating his position in the Sudan and Arabia he intervenes in Crete (1823) and on the mainland of Greece (1825), nominally on behalf of his Ottoman overlord. He nearly succeeds in crushing the revolution, until Britain, France and Russia combine to defeat him at the naval battle of Navarino, off Pylos (1827).

### The Modern Greek State

**1830** Independence achieved for southern Greece.

**1834** Athens, then with a population of 6, 000, becomes capital of Greece (Nauplia and Aegina have earlier enjoyed this honour),

British and French fleets control piracy, and stability returns to the Aegean.

**1881** Thessaly and Epirus returned from Turkey to Greece.

**1912-13** A Balkan war gives Greece the opportunity to recapture Macedonia and the North Aegean islands.

**1916** Greece enters the First World War on the side of the Allies: Turkey sides with Germany.

**1921-22** Greece takes advantage of Turkey's defeat to invade, with the aim of 'liberating' all the Greek-speaking lands of Asia

Minor. The plan misfires, as the Turks under Kemal Ataturk drive the Greeks 'back into the sea'. Hundreds of thousands of Greek civilians massacred in Turkey. The Greek king abdicates, and his government falls. A military junta negotiates a vast exchange of populations. More than 1 million refugees resettled in Greece many on Aegean islands. Smaller numbers of Turkish-speaking Greeks removed to Turkey.

**1940** Italian, and then German, troops occupy Greece during the Second World War.

**1945** Allied Victory leads to the return of the Dodecanese from Italy.

**1947** A civil war eventually resolves in Conservative governments and outlawing of the Communist Party.

**1965** Election of a Liberal government under George Papandreou precipitates a constitutional struggle with the Monarchy, leading to:

**1967** The Colonels' Military Coup. A Junta suppresses democracy for seven years, until ended by student riots and, more immediately, Turkish invasion of the northern part of Cyprus.

**1974** Election of a Conservative government under Constantine Karamanlis.

**1980** Karamanlis elected President.

**1981** Socialist government of PASOK party under Andreas Papandreou.

**1986** Greece joins the European Economic Community.

KAVALA

KERAMOTI

THASSOPOULA

C. Pachis

Skala
Rachoni

Glyfada

Limenas

Makriammos

Rachoni

Skala
Prinos

Skala
Sotiros

Prinos

Panagia

Chrisi
Ammoudia

Potamia

Skala
Kalirachis

Sotiros

M⊙ Ag.
Panteleimon

Mt.
Ipsarion ▲1204

Skala
Potamias

Kalirachi

Maries

Kastro

Theologos

Kinira

Skala
Maries

Kalivia

Limenaria

C. Kefalas

Pefkari

Tripiti

Potos

M
Archangelou

Aliki

Psili
Ammos

N

THASSOS

0          5 km

For legend see page 35

TEN

# Thassos

*Population: 13,111*     *Highest point 1204m*
*Area: 379 sq km*       *Hotel beds: about 4100*

Thassos is the most northerly island in the Aegean and also one of the closest to the mainland, separated at the nearest point by a mere 12 kilometres of sheltered water. Seen from Kavala, the island seems to block off the south east approach to the port. Thassos has always been important: because of its gold and other minerals; because of its abundant and unfailing water resources; because of its ability to control or to disrupt the Egnatian Way, the main east-west highway with Asia, linking Rome and Constantinople; and it is altogether too near the mainland to be ignored. While most of the North Aegean islands are green and well wooded, the forests of Thassos, which cover about half the island, are renowned for their greenness and luxuriance. The centre of the island is mountainous, but the mountains are not so steep as to be impenetrable. There are substantial areas of low-lying fertile land around much of the coast, as well as in some of the long mountain valleys.

The summer climate of Thassos is good, but not typical of the Aegean. Its proximity to the mainland, especially to the mountains behind Kavala, shields it from the *meltemi,* the prevailing cool, dry wind. As a result, it usually lacks the invigorating freshness of most other islands.

For many years the people of Thessaloniki and other northern Greek towns have been flocking to Thassos during their summer holidays, even for short weekends. As a result the resorts have grown up steadily, with an absence of large brash new developments. One estimate suggests there are as many as half a million visitors to the island each year, although this is surely an exaggeration. But the number of Greeks enjoying holidays in Thassos is certainly large. Conversely, the island has been less accessible than many other Greek islands to tourists from northern Europe: it has no airport, and Kavala Airport on the mainland has only recently become international. This, and the preponderance of smaller hotels, makes Thassos unattractive to the big package tour operators. Individual foreigners do come, mostly overland through Yugoslavia, but the majority of holiday-makers are Greek. Thus, most cooking is in the Greek style, and prices are realistic. On the other hand, few concessions are yet made to the foreigner. Most signs are in Greek only, and most people even in the tourist industry speak only Greek.

## Arrival by sea

The chief departure port for Thassos island is Kavala, with a journey time of one hour. During the winter there are six daily trips in each direction, rising in summer to about 20. The ferry arrives at Skala Prinos, a very small port some 16kms west of the capital. A few sailings continue on to the capital, but it is as quick to disembark at Skala Prinos and continue by bus or private transport.

The alternative departure point is Keramoti, a small low-lying village 45kms by road to the south east of Kavala. From here ferries travel direct to the capital, with a journey time of 35 minutes. Minimum frequency is six trips daily, rising to a peak of over 20.

All the ships involved are drive-on/drive-off car ferries of the landing craft type. The principal operator is the Thassos Steamship Company, with four modern vessels (Thassos I, II, III & IV). Capacity varies from 300-750 passengers, and from 40-85 cars. The company runs services all the year round on both routes. When the volume of traffic justifies it, two other smaller operators join in, with the effect of increasing the frequency of sailings. Bogdanis has a comparable ship to the Thassos class on the Kavala/Skala Prinos route, and three smaller ships run a shuttle from the capital to Keramoti. The published timing of sailings cannot be relied on during the high season, when ships tend to leave as soon as loaded.

Fares of all operators are the same. Foot passengers pay at an office on the dockside. Motorists pay on boarding, and the vehicle fare includes the driver. Fares from Keramoti average about 70% of those from Kavala, but the saving is probably cancelled out by the cost of extra driving. However at peak periods waiting times should be shorter from Keramoti. There may also be a greater number of departures.

*Kavala harbour. This kind of ferry — of the landing craft type — is widely used in Greece for short trips. Passengers can remain in their cars if they wish. In the view below, the Byzantine castle can be clearly seen, and fishing caiques line the inner quayside, convenient to the fish market.*

Neither island port offers secure berthing in all weathers. Consequently the ferry service is sometimes suspended during the winter, perhaps ten times a year on average. Summer services are rarely affected. Because of the frequency of car ferry services, and the moderate fares charged, caiques play little part in the transport system of the island.

There are no onward scheduled ferry services from the island, although the ships from Kavala pass very close to the west of Thassos on their way to Lemnos.

*Limenas. Behind the fishing port and the strip of shops and restaurants which border it can be found the ruins of the ancient Agora or market place, now carefully conserved. In the past many priceless relics were carried off, often merely for re-use as building material.*

# Road system

Thassos enjoys an excellent road network. A good tarmac road runs right round the island. Tarmac spurs, sometimes of surprisingly generous dimensions in relation to the volume of traffic, run up to a number of inland villages. Others give access to beaches. Signposting is good, except in the capital. In addition there are a few sections of unsurfaced all-weather road, as well as more than 200kms of forest track. The more important of these, giving access to isolated mountain communities, are perfectly usable in summer by ordinary cars. Others are rougher, more suitable for trucks and four-wheel drive. The more important unsurfaced roads are signposted to some extent, but only in Greek.

**Buses** The bus service, administered from Kavala, is comprehensive and frequent. All villages on tarmac roads enjoy a service. Between the towns and ports the frequency of service approaches once an hour in summer. In addition, five services daily run a complete clockwise circuit of the island, starting from the capital. Times and destinations are usually displayed at bus stops.

**Taxis** The island has many taxis, which may be found waiting in any of the towns and main villages. Many are equipped with two-way radio, and so can respond quickly to a telephone call.

**Petrol** There are plenty of filling stations on the coast road in the north and west of the island. Most sell diesel fuel. But in the south-east and east there is a 44km section between Potos and the capital without any filling stations at all.

# Centres of population

Thassos has a variety of places with shops and other facilities, which differ widely in size and atmosphere. Two are, by islands standards, towns, with schools, offices and banks. Others are villages, large, medium and small, whose character depends on the extent to which they are in contact with the modern world, and especially whether they are situated on the coast or in the mountains. The names of several coastal villages are prefixed Skala (which means landing steps or similar), indicating that they originated as an outpost for another village in the hills, expanding when the decline of piracy permitted people to live safely on the coast, convenient for working the fields and fishing.

**Thassos town (Limenas/Limen)** is the capital and chief town, but unfortunately the naming is a bit confusing. Thassos is now an official designation, but this name causes confusion with the island itself. The islanders usually call it Limenas, but the visitor finds this too similar to Limenaria, the (only) name of the island's second town. To add to the difficulty, the road signs read Limen. Tourists must therefore be prepared to react appropriately to all three names.

*Limenas. Part of the ancient city wall below the Greek theatre, showing one of the ten gates. Note the very large blocks of stone used in its construction.*

The town once covered a much greater area than it does today. Nevertheless, its layout and infrastructure are not well adapted to its function as chief town. The present day focus is the new waterfront, where ferries berth, and vehicles queue to board them. Here are the police station (including tourist police), government offices, hotels and restaurants. Immediately behind, the main shopping street runs parallel to it. Other shopping streets radiate inland. An anti-clockwise oneway traffic system operates in the immediate approaches to the waterfront.

Limenas is interesting for its historical associations and should certainly be visited. It has most of the facilities expected of the chief town of an important island, including a cinema, disco, and rental of cars and motorbikes. For the antiquities, see under Cultural interest. See also under Beaches.

**Limenaria** and its immediate surroundings will probably, however, be more to the taste of tourists from northern Europe planning to stay any length of time on the island. This is the second town of the island, and dedicated entirely to tourism. The main road runs behind the town, allowing local traffic to mingle fairly harmlessly with the holidaymakers. Parking space can usually be found.

Until the middle of the nineteenth century the site was virtually unoccupied. Then the inhabitants of the isolated fortress village of Kastro felt safe enough to abandon their inconvenient location to found a new village. This was substantially enlarged at the beginning of the twentieth century, when a German company built a large plant for processing the metal ores mined nearby. Its substantial remains can be seen today over the hill to the south of the town. The ruins of the company's very impressive office block — known as the Palataki (little palace) — stand forlornly on the headland overlooking the harbour.

The town has a number of smaller sized hotels. There are many cafés and restaurants, often with tables spread out to the very edge of the beach. The small fishing port is attractive, and an adjoining pier serves as carpark and centre for boat trips.

## Other towns

**Potamia** and **Panagia** are large villages on the sides of a horseshoe of hills, overlooking the great Bay of Potamia. The hills continue to rise steeply behind, towards Mount Ipsarion, the highest point of the island. Potamia, now bypassed by the main road, is of little interest to the tourist. Panagia, for a few years in the 1840s the centre of administration of the island, is a different matter. It is a charming little village, with many traditional buildings set in narrow streets which twist steeply up the hillside. Running water abounds in the central open spaces. Unfortunately the main road still passes through the lower part of the village, although there are signs of a future bypass. In spite of this, the place is lively in a dignified way, especially in the evening. There are no hotels, but discerning holidaymakers can stay in immaculately kept private houses, and descend by bus or taxi to enjoy the nearby beaches.

In the early nineteenth century **Theologos** was the island's centre of administration. It remains a large village, with a variety of older buildings clustered around a single long narrow street. A modern road runs above the village, terminating for the moment at the cemetery — there are plans eventually to extend it to the coast. From above, there is a pleasing uniformity of mellowed stone slate roofs. The bare grey hillside behind is dotted with the black, white and brown of grazing goats. Below are the lush greens of fruit trees and vegetable gardens.

The traditional houses of the village can be admired. One larger one has been carefully restored, calls itself the Popularity Museum, and contains an exhibition of handwoven wall carpets. (If closed, the villagers will know where to find the custodian.) The churches are also worth visiting. But the special atmosphere of Theologos is due to its water — water from springs and streams cunningly channelled to trickle through the streets, before descending to irrigate the gardens· water which splashes with reckless abandon from communal taps; water which runs clear and cold on even the hottest day.

Most of the other accessible inland villages will be of little interest to the tourist, except as starting points for forest expeditions. **Sotir** (Sotiros), perhaps, is different. It is a very small village, built on a steep slope with narrow cobbled streets. For better or worse, little has been done to change it in recent years. There is a pleasant and shady taverna situated beside a splashing fountain. The bus stops at the entrance to the village, where cars should also be left.

*Boat trips from Limenaria take holidaymakers to see the Mount Athos peninsula, the most easterly prong of the Chalcidice. It is not possible to go ashore but there are more than a dozen important monasteries clearly visible from the boat.*

# Accommodation

### Hotels on Thassos

| Class | Name | | Rooms | Tel. (code 0593) |
|---|---|---|---|---|
| **At Limenas** | | | | |
| A | Roula | Apartments | 6 | 22905 |
| A | Amfipolis | | 47 | (NYK) |
| B | Timoleon | | 30 | 22177 |
| B | Xenia | | 27 | 22105 |
| B | Poseidon | (Pension) | 16 | 22690 |
| B | Akti | (Pension) | 15 | 22326 |
| B | Diamanto | (Pension) | 16 | 22622 |
| B | Dionyssos | (Pension) | 11 | 22198 |
| B | Elli-Maria | (Pension) | 20 | 23133 |
| B | Gallini | (Pension) | 16 | 22195 |
| B | Georgios | (Pension) | 12 | 22333 |
| B | Mary | (Pension) | 9 | 22257 |
| B | Viky | (Pension) | 13 | 22314 |
| B | Villa Nysteri | (Pension) | 10 | 22055 |
| C | Alcyon | | 11 | 22148 |
| C | Angelika | | 26 | 22387 |
| C | Laios | | 27 | 22309 |
| C | Lido | | 18 | 22929 |
| C | Panorama | | 8 | 22585 |
| C | Villa Meresi | | 20 | 22410 |
| C | Kihos | (Apartments) | 8 | 22469 |
| C | Olga | (Apartments) | 4 | 22415 |
| **At Makriammos** | | | | |
| A | Makriammos | (Bungalows) | 206 | 22101 |
| **At Glyfada** | | | | |
| C | Glyfada | | 52 | 22164 |
| **At Panaghia** | | | | |
| B | Chryfis | (Pension) | 9 | 61451 |
| **At Skala Potamias** | | | | |
| B | Kamelia | (Pension) | 15 | 61463 |
| B | Miramare | | 25 | 61040 |
| C | Atlantis | | 8 | 61490 |
| C | Blue Sea | | 12 | 61482 |

**At Skala Potamias (continued)**

| | | | | |
|---|---|---|---|---|
| C | Arion | | 7 | 61525 |
| C | Korina | | 30 | (NYK) |

**At Kinyra**

| | | | | |
|---|---|---|---|---|
| C | Gerda | | 12 | 61482 |

**At Potos**

| | | | | |
|---|---|---|---|---|
| C | Olympion | | 54 | 51930 |

**At Pefkari**

| | | | | |
|---|---|---|---|---|
| B | Kappa-Hi | (Pension) | 23 | 51568 |

**At Limenaria**

| | | | | |
|---|---|---|---|---|
| B | Thalassies | (Pension) | 21 | 51163 |
| C | Menel | | 18 | 51396 |
| C | Sgouridis | | 14 | 51241 |

**At Skala Prinos**

| | | | | |
|---|---|---|---|---|
| B | Elektra | (Pension) | 18 | 71374 |
| B | Europa | (Pension) | 12 | 71212 |
| B | Oasis | (Pension) | 10 | (NYK) |

**At Dasyllion**

| | | | | |
|---|---|---|---|---|
| C | Crystal | | 13 | 71272 |

**At Skala Rachoni**

| | | | | |
|---|---|---|---|---|
| C | Hara | | 7 | 71296 |

and 47 other lower category hotels.

**Private accommodation** This is widely available in the towns and larger villages. Tourist Offices have details, and there are also many individual 'To Let' notices. See also under Walks and excursions — Kastro.

# Camping

Thassos is well provided with campsites. Three are already in operation, and two more (at Cape Prinos and Potos) are under construction.

**Camping Ioannidis** (tel. (0593) 71377) is situated at 2kms from Skala Prinos, on the road to the capital. It's the largest and best run site on the island with more than 180 individual pitches, and more projected. There's a good private sandy beach, with mature pine trees immediately behind, a good restaurant, and a shop stocking camping gas. There are trees supplemented by artificial shade. Open from 1 May to mid October.

**Pefkari Camping** (tel. (0593) 51595) is situated beside an excellent private beach. It's a small, quality site, with attractive stone built buildings for the facilities. There are some mature olive trees, with many more trees recently planted. However, lacking individual pitches, the site can become uncomfortably crowded. Open April to October.

**Golden Beach Camping** (tel. (0593) 61472) is situated beside the public beach at Chrisi Ammoudia. Trees have been planted, but there will be little shade before they mature. There's also a shortage of electric points. The site — 1½ hectares and due to be doubled — is owned by the Panagia Municipality. Organisation is informal, but prices are cheap. Open May to September.

There are also a number of unofficial sites, fields or olive groves belonging to private individuals. Prices would be about half those charged by official campsites.

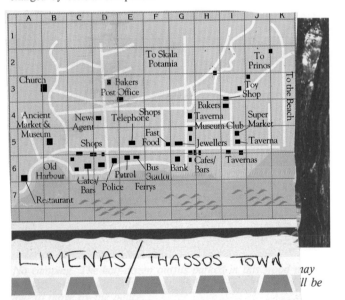

Thassos is ideal for free camping outside the main holiday season. But in July and August very large numbers of intending campers arrive, many with tents, and others planning to sleep in lorries, vans and pickups. Free camping is, of course, against the law, and almost all the most suitable places have prominent No Camping notices. However, free camping is tolerated on waste ground behind the central part of the long beach at Potamia Bay — access is easier from the south. Elsewhere free camping takes place widely, but campers must be prepared for the possibility of being asked to move on by the police.

Water is found in every town and village from communal taps and fountains. Camping Gas is usually stocked in Limenas and Limenaria, but supplies sell out quickly during the season and there may be a considerable time lapse before fresh stocks become available. At this time, the shop at Camping Ioannidis offers the best chance.

## Beaches

Much of the coastline is accessible from the main road, and a wide variety of beaches can be found. Starting from the capital, and travelling clockwise around the island, these are some of the main beaches:

**Limenas** The town beaches are sandy and quite satisfactory, except that they are often overcrowded.

**Makriammos** Although this is probably the best sandy beach on the island, this fact is unfortunately of academic interest to the ordinary tourist for the beach and its approaches are completely shut off, and remain the private preserve of a high class bungalow hotel complex. There are some smaller beaches to the south, but access is difficult except by boat.

**Bay of Potamias** The beach extends the full width of the bay, some 3kms of mostly fine white sand. It is easily reached from its two extremities, where small holiday resorts have developed. The beach at Chrisi Ammoudia in the north is particularly attractive, and facilities include fresh water showers. Skala Potamias to the south has shops as well as a number of small hotels and restaurants, but a section of its beach is stony.

**Kinyra** has several small hotels and a pleasant restaurant. The nearer beaches are narrow and rather stony, and the better ones beyond difficult to reach except by boat. As the road descends towards Aliki, some good small beaches can be seen far below, but are difficult to reach.

**Aliki** itself has the most delightful small beaches on the island, but since its attractions are so visible from above, it gets very crowded in high season. Two small bays back onto a narrow spit of sand planted with olive trees, which shelter a few fishing cottages and a taverna. A short distance beyond, opposite the junction of the track to Thimonia, a small isolated beach may be used by naturists.

Below the monastery of **Archangelou** (see Cultural) the sea makes a dramatic indentation into the steep cliffs. Far below lies a good sandy beach, well sheltered and suitable for use early and late in the season, and also used by naturists. The south west undoubtedly contains the best and most extensive grouping of beaches on the island. **Psili Ammos** has good sand and some rock. **Potos,** once the port of Theologos, has developed into a small modern resort attractive to foreigners. It is surrounded by sandy beaches. **Pefkari** has excellent sandy beaches, and as its name implies, pine trees come

*Pefkari beach. A boat party from Llmenaria is just arriving to swell the numbers on this secluded sandy beach. The beach-side taverna serves lunch.*

right down to the water's edge. There are several small beaches to the east of **Limenaria,** not too easy to get at. The town beach has been somewhat encroached on by buildings, but there is a freshwater shower. A large expanse of sand continues to the west, but is partly private to the Stelakis Restaurant (with accommodation). Close to Cape Kefalas, **Tripiti,** also sandy, has an attractively situated taverna.

**Skala Maries, Skala Kalirachis** and **Skala Sotiros** are sm holiday resorts with adequate sandy beaches. The former is muc more interesting than it appears from the main road, and ne developments are in progress.

From Cape Prinos to **Skala Rachoni** the shoreline is featureless with more or less continuous sand. **Skala Prinos,** where the ferries berth, has a number of restaurants and shops, as well as a yard for building and repairing caiques. Elsewhere along the coast tavernas are found in the more favoured spots. There are fine views of the mainland from Cape Pachis. From here back to Limenas the road runs close to the shore. Beaches are usually stony, the few stretches of sand monopolised by isolated hotels and restaurants.

# Agriculture and products

Although tourism is today the chief activity of Thassos, agriculture and forestry continue to be important, especially for the economies of the inland villages. Some 20 per cent of the area, effectively most of the lower lying and accessible land, is planted with olives. The trees are well cared for, and regularly harvested, for pressing at several plants on the island.

In former times sufficient wheat was grown for the island's needs, but abandoned millstones can often be seen, whilst flour now arrives in sacks from the mainland. The more marginal of the small terraced fields are no longer cultivated, providing at the most fodder for the many sheep, goats and donkeys.

Aristotle and Virgil both praised the wine of Thassos in classical times. Today most of what little wine is made goes for private consumption. A very sweet red wine, made near Kalirachi, is sold in some shops, but cannot be recommended with much enthusiasm. The local Ouzo, on the other hand, is smooth and delicate, rivalling that of Lesbos. Wine labelled Tharsos, by the way, comes from the mainland, near Thessaloniki.

The villagers grow excellent fruit and vegetables on their small plots, but the shops are more cheaply stocked from the mainland. But the island does specialise in walnuts. Many trees have been planted, especially near the river beds. These form the basis for a considerable cottage industry, in combination with the other island speciality, honey. The nuts are mixed with honey in various ways — whole, pieces, ground up, and so on. They are then filled into one kilo tins with distinctive coloured labels, which are then sold all over the island and also on the mainland. Impossible for the foreigner to tell exactly what is inside, but he can ask for the lid to be taken off to view the contents. The product is intended to be eaten just as it is, with a teaspoon.

Bees are kept on most Greek islands, but nowhere more than on Thassos. They are found in huge colonies of a hundred hives or more, at frequent intervals along the roads and forest tracks. The bees must be a very docile strain, since the beekeepers open up the hives and take the honey without any protective clothing whatever! Honey is of excellent quality, and on sale everywhere at reasonable prices.

**Forestry** About half the area of the island is actively managed as forest. The pine trees are cut for building timber and wood pulp. Surprisingly, there seems to be no attempt to tap the resin, as in the Sporades. In spite of the very great fire risk, it is accepted that the forests will and should be used for recreation.

**Minerals** Thassos has always been noted for its marble, which continues to be exported in quantity. The ancient Thassians used vast amounts to build their city, even lining the floor of the harbour with it. They did not have to look far to find it. Indeed some whole mountains appear to be composed of solid marble. The earliest mineral to be extracted was gold, but the Phoenicians and Thracians took most of that. The best lodes were found near Kinyra.

Large amounts of copper, cadmium, iron and zinc were mined in the past. There undoubtedly remain huge amounts of minerals, which may one day come into their own. But the most notable discovery in recent years has been oil. This lies under the sea to the north west, and rigs can clearly be seen out to sea. The oilfield, the first in Greek waters, has been productive since 1981 and currently contributes about seven per cent of Greece's requirements. Fortunately pollution has not so far been a problem. The product is taken to a refinery east of Kavala for processing. Ownership of this oilfield, and even more so of some unexplored fields believed to exist close to it, is of course a major source of dispute between Greece and Turkey.

# Historical background

### Early History
The first settlers probably reached Thassos before 3000BC. They were certainly present on the nearest mainland well before that time, and it seems that their nomadic predecessors understood rudimentary seafaring. But legend relates that the island was named after a certain Thassos, a Phoenician. He came to these parts in search of his sister, Europa: she had been abducted by the lascivious Zeus, disguised for the occasion as a bull. Unsuccessful in his search, Thassos was content to settle instead on the island.

### Phoenicians and Thracians
There is independent evidence to confirm that the Phoenicians were among the early settlers. They brought with them the worship of Herakles (Hercules), which continued for a long time afterwards. Later the Thracians colonised the island, probably to secure its gold. At that time, following the fashion set by Troy, gold and silver drinking goblets were an indispensable status symbol for chieftains.

### The Greeks arrive
At the beginning of the seventh century BC the first 'Greeks' arrived. They were from Paros in the Cyclades, and they came to found a new colony, in obedience to the oracle of Apollo at Delphi. Their chief was Telesikles, and it did not take them long to capture the island. We know quite a lot about this expedition, since Telesikles' son was one Archilochos, a poet in his own time nearly as famous as Homer and the inventor of Iambic verse. At first he did not think much of Thassos. "This place sticks up like a donkey's back, crowned with wild woods", he wrote. And again "There is no good land here". Moreover the gold of Thassos was found to be nearly exhausted, and there was a great need for fresh reserves. Fortunately there were goldfields on the mainland opposite — on Mt. Pangeon behind Kavala and elsewhere. But the problem was first to drive off the Thracians who were already exploiting them. Archilochos took part in the first expedition, which was defeated. He ran away, thus living to fight another day, but had to throw away his shield in order to run fast enough. Such conduct was 'not done', so if it was, one did not brag about it! But Archilochos wrote to a friend:

> Some Thracian flaunts the shield I left behind,
> My trusty shield — I had to — in a wood.
> Well, I have saved my life; so never mind
> That shield; I'll get another just as good,

perhaps the first known occasion in literature when the author himself takes the part of anti-hero. Eventually the Thassians managed to drive away the Thracians. Their possessions on the mainland grew, and became known as the Continent of Thassos.

## Persian invasions

Thus Thassos found itself a rich little island, but its position was difficult. Situated so close to the mainland, no invader could ignore the island; but it was so accessible that any powerful invader could reduce it at will. Such a threat came from Persia at the beginning of the fifth century BC. The first invasion was in 490 BC, when the Thassians resisted bravely. As a result they lost their entire fleet, and suffered the destruction of the city walls. The Persians were turned back at the Battle of Marathon, but came again in 480, under the personal command of Xerxes, their new King. In no condition to withstand another siege, this time the Thassians tried different tactics. They fed the enemy troops, as they would be expected to do anyway, but also prepared a great feast for Xerxes and his entire army. The cost, says Herodotus, was 400 talents, more than one complete year's income from the gold mines.

## The end of Thasian independence

Xerxes was finally defeated at Salamis, and Thassos was press-ganged into joining the Delian league, which had been created by Athens to share the burden of keeping the peace. Soon, feeling stronger, and smarting under the burden of contributions, Thassos seceded from the League. That gave Athens the excuse it was looking for. Kimon attacked the island, and after a siege of two years, took it. Afterwards Thassos continued to have commercial success, even issuing its own coins, which have been found all over the Mediterranean. But its political independence was virtually finished.

In 359 BC Philip II became King of Macedonia. He had great ambitions, and quickly appreciated his need for money to fulfil them. He chose his moment with great skill, waiting until rival states were preoccupied, then advancing on the Continent of Thassos, he took the Pangeon goldmine, and founded his own settlement of

Philippi. He exploited the mine with vigour, and soon it was yielding 1000 talents a year — sufficient means to unlock many a city gate. Soon Thassos was itself absorbed into Macedonia.

In 196 BC it became part of the Roman Empire. Rome was particularly anxious for the active support of the Thassians, and gave the island generous privileges. For a period it led an island republic which included the Sporades. When the Romans lost a battle at Philippi, the defeated troops were given safe refuge in Thassos.

As part of the Byzantine Empire, Thassos did not prosper. The Gateluzzi family from Genoa acquired it, but were forced to barter it to the Turks in 1455. There followed a period of severe decline. From 1770-1774 the island belonged to Russia, during the attempt of Catherine the Great to secure a foothold in the Mediterranean.

### 1813 to the present

From 1813 the history of Thassos becomes rather unusual. Mehemet Ali Pasha had become Governor of Egypt. Nominally he was subject to the Sultan of Turkey, who was now looking for a means of rewarding his overpowerful vassal, in the hope of securing his loyalty in the future. Mehemet Ali had been born in Kavala; his statue can be seen in the town, and also his house. Ali asked to be given Thassos, and the Sultan duly obliged. Thus Thassos became the personal fief of the ruler of Egypt. In the early years Egyptian rule was enlightened, with a substantial amount of autonomy. In the 1820s the island did join in the general Greek uprising, and succeeded in having all the Turkish population removed from the island. Later Egyptian rule was more restrictive, and in 1902 the island reverted briefly to Turkey. It was at this time that the German Spiedel Company established its mining operations around Limenaria. But in 1912, during the Balkan Wars, the opportunity was taken to reunite the island with Greece.

# Cultural interest

The capital of Thassos (Limenas, Limen) is built on the site of the ancient settlement and the remains of the ancient Greek city take pride of place. Surrounding the modern town, and mostly stretching up into the hills behind, are the partly preserved ancient walls, built of marble in the fifth century and further fortified with defensive towers. Ten of the original gateways to these impressive ramparts have been traced but it is the Gate of Silenius, with its satyr, which can be seen at the junction of the road to Makriammos, that is the best preserved and of most interest to the tourist.

### The Acropolis
On top of the hill behind the port stands the Acropolis, with a temple to Athena nearby. Access is by footpath only. On the way up the ancient theatre is passed, superbly sited, like most of its kind, with splendid views across the bay. During July and August dramas are given in the theatre under the auspices of the Philippi and Thassos Festival. The North Greek State Theatre and other companies present performances mostly from the Greek classics. However, it should be remembered before buying tickets that the climb to the theatre is entirely by footpath. On a hot summer's evening this activity is not for the elderly or infirm.

### Harbour and Museum
The ancient harbour was, essentially, the present fishing harbour. Behind the restaurants now lining the waterfront can be seen substantial remains of the Agora or market place, together with several temples. Nearby is the Museum, containing objects remaining after the Louvre and the National Museum at Thessaloniki had taken their pick. Well worth a visit (closed Tuesdays, entrance free on Thursdays and Sundays).

### Outside the city centre
On the outskirts of the town are further remains — The Temple of Hercules, the Hermes and Fairies Gate — but many of these less accessible vestiges of the past are obscured by the encroachments of nature and the activities of man, and persistence of devotees of culture is needed to find and appreciate them.

In Theologos, at the end of July and beginning of August there are representations of the traditional Thassian wedding ceremony. Easter celebrations reach their peak on the Tuesday after Easter.

## Walks and excursions

Thassos has four monasteries in good order, of which two — M.Archangelou and Agios Panteleimon — are still functioning.
● **M.Archangelou** monastery stands directly beside the main coast road, behind a high wall, and cannot be missed. It is in fact a nunnery, belonging to the Mount Athos monastic State. Many

tourists on their circuit of the island stop to have a look at it. Dress regulations are unusually strict, but women can hire long skirts (which may have to serve as shawls to cover bare arms). Long jeans are also available for men arriving in shorts. A small church can be seen, but the main cell block is presently closed for restoration. Admission is free, but a small donation is expected from those not hiring clothing.

● **Agios Panteleimon** (1½hrs from Kalirachi) By contrast this monastery, which houses a mixed religious community, is situated in splendid isolation up in the hills. The normal route starts at Prinos, but the route with the shortest unsurfaced part starts at Kalirachi (turn sharp left on entering the village square, on to a forest track).

**Limenas.** *The ancient theatre is used during the summer festival. But a visit is recommended in any season, despite the steepness of the path (walking is the only means of getting there). The view is stunning and nearby a well-preserved section of city wall (5th century BC) is worth inspecting.*

● **Profitis Ilias** (1 hr) Disused, but a straightforward walk from Theologos. The fork from the main forest track is signposted. Splendid views over the east coast.
● **M.Panagias** Easily found a short distance south of the Maries road, but of little interest.

## The south

The south of the island, although hilly, is less so than the north. Those two requirements for survival against pirates — a high defensible position, and a reliable water supply — are less easily found there. One such place is **Kastro,** which eventually provided refuge for most of the south (Theologos had its own sanctuary). It is most easily approached from Limenaria. A rough forest track, signposted, starts at Kalivia. The walk is straightforward — indeed the track is probably suitable for ordinary cars. The Kastro is on a high rocky pinnacle, with steep falls on three sides. Close by are some 30 houses, from the village abandoned in the nineteenth century (see Limenaria). Until recently it was derelict, except for the church, which would have been cared for, and opened once a year on its Saint's day. Beside the church, a spring flows continuously. It seems a miracle that water can emerge at such a high spot, but no doubt there is a scientific explanation! However, some of the houses have now been put in order, and it is possible for tourists to be accommodated there; but — beware! — it is spartan and suited only to those fairly tough types for whom the novelty is likely to outweigh the lack of physical comforts and conveniences. The custodian runs a do-it-yourself taverna.

Further inland still, the high mountain hamlets of **Votos, Gemma, Spathi** and others can be discovered by the intrepid.

## Mount Athos

Boat trips run from Limenaria to see the famous **Mount Athos** peninsula. It was established by edict of the Byzantine Emperor in 1060 as a self-governing monastic republic (Agion Oros), its secular relationship with the Greek State being similar to that of the Vatican with Italy. An earlier edict in 885 had recognised it as a preserve solely for monks, although they had probably been present in the area several centuries previously. The first monastery was traditionally founded in 963, and eventually there were some 40 monasteries with up to 1000 monks in each. Even after the fall of the Byzantine Empire, the republic remained the spiritual centre of Orthodoxy. Indeed it was not until the Greek Wars of Independence, when the monks antagonised the Turks by supporting the rest of Greece, that real decline set in. This has continued during the twentieth century, with some 20 monasteries housing fewer than 2000 monks in all now remaining open.

The presence of women, and even female animals, has always been forbidden, but until recently men could visit quite easily. However, numbers increased so much that bureaucratic obstacles have had to be introduced. But many of the monasteries can quite clearly be seen from the boat. Naturally, tourists are unable to land.

Other boat excursions can be made from Limenaria. The main excursion from Limenas is to the island of **Thassopoula,** which has a special reputation for its snakes.

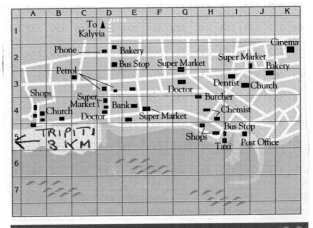

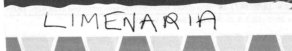

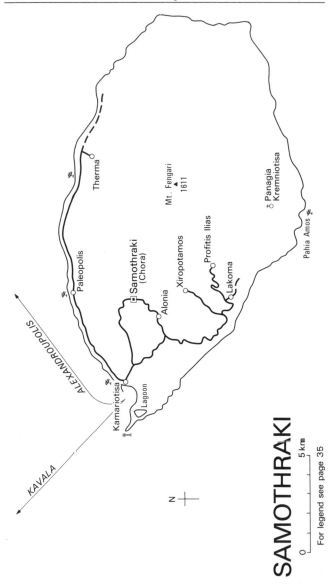

SAMOTHRAKI

For legend see page 35

0 ___ 5 km

ELEVEN

# Samothraki

*Population: 2,871        Highest point: 1611m*
*Area: 178 sq. kms       Hotel beds: about 275*

Samothraki (Samothrace) is a very mountainous island indeed. By
far the greater part of it is taken up with high hills and mountains,
rising above 1600 metres. The ancient geographer Strabo wrote that
it resembled an upturned woman's breast. Today those jagged
ridges of bare rock seem far removed from any part of the female
anatomy. Maybe in his day the mountain tops looked different,
beneath a decent coverage of forest. Or perhaps he never actually
saw the island for himself!

   The small amount of lower lying land can be considered in three
parts. In the western extremity there is an expanse of rolling
wheatfields. Along the north coast the wheatfields give way to
scrub, and eventually to quite substantial areas of plane forest. On
the south coast the wheatfields are progessively replaced by olive
groves as the land becomes steeper until eventually the plunging
slopes become unusable.

   At one time the island attracted only visitors with an interest in
classical antiquities. The archeological site is certainly impressive,
and also in some respects unique. But the majority of summer
holidaymakers who pack the ferries to overcapacity care little for
antiquities. As the choice for a summer holiday, Samothraki is
windy, and therefore inevitably dusty. In many parts there is no
shade. Compared with some other islands, the beaches seem
unimpressive. There are no water sports, nor indeed sport of any
kind, except for mountaineers and cross-country motorbiking
specialists.

   But the tourists certainly come, although one must not give the
impression that tourism is a major industry. Just one ferry crossing
to Thassos carries more tourists in a day than all the ferries

Samothraki can manage in a week. And on the credit side, the local people are friendly and tolerant, and the police keep a low profile. The island has plenty of water, and a few parts are well shaded. It seems that people come here to make do with less than perfect facilities, because they can get away from mass tourism and do their own thing.

## Arrival by sea

The main departure port is Alexandroupolis. From here the Samothraki Shipping Company operates a small conventional car ferry, which shuttles to and fro to give a daily service in each direction throughout much of the year. During summer, frequency is increased by squeezing in a second sailing on five days of the week. The ferry is called 'Saos' after the highest peak of Mount Fengari. The 'Saos' is of Baltic origin, elderly but adequately comfortable. The journey takes 3 hours.

There are also occasional ferries from Kavala. In 1988 a small car ferry called 'Arsinoe', with agents in Thessaloniki, was plying the route two or more times each week (4 hours). In consequence, presumably, the long-standing weekly service from Loucas Nomicos was in abeyance at the start of the tourist season. In previous years their car ferry Skopelos had come up from Kavala once weekly, and continued to Samothraki and Alexandroupolis, before returning to Lemnos via Samothraki and Kavala. This illustrated one of the commercial realities of Greek ferries. On a clear day Lemnos can easily be seen from the south coast of Samothraki. At one time Loucas Nomicos did operate a direct link, taking some three hours. But so few local people travel between the two islands that, in spite of representations by the NTOG on behalf of tourism, an intermediate call at Kavala was introduced. The journey time between Samothraki and Lemnos is now 10 hours, but the service is more profitable that way.

All the companies maintain separate ticket offices on the waterfronts of Alexandroupolis and Kamariotisa (the port of Samothraki). Passenger fares are identical, but for vehicles Loucas Nomicos is slightly cheaper, it is said because of its government subsidy. The motorist is warned that conditions for embarkation at Alexandroupolis are unusually chaotic. By contrast, on the island there is good control.

The summer schedule of 'Saos' gives the possibility of making a day trip to the island. This would allow some 9 hours for sightseeing, which is certainly sufficient to see the archeological site and the capital.

## Road system

At the time of the author's last visit, the island was in the throes of a major road improvement programme. Much of the network had already been widened and realigned, and awaited only a top-dressing of tarmac to convert into good motor road. This final stage was said to be imminent, and already reflected in the local tourist map.

All principal roads converge on Kamariotisa. One runs along most of the north coast, closely following the shoreline. A second road, already tarmac, runs inland to the capital. From this road, a third one forks right after 1km to give access to the villages in the south, which are all inland. In addition a concrete road runs down from the capital to Alonia, and an extension connects with the southern road.

**Buses** The island enjoys a good bus service, which is provided from Alexandroupolis. There are three buses, which virtually cover the entire road network. Services are geared to the arrival and departure of ferries. At the peak, there are eight daily services to the capital and Therma, and four to Profitis Ilias which also call at Alonia. Buses can be criticised for usually failing to display their destination. Alternatively, the destination shown is misleading, such as Alexandroupolis, or Topikon — which means Local.

Taxis There are several taxis, which can usually be found waiting in the port.

**Petrol** Petrol and diesel fuel can be obtained in the port only.

## Centres of population

The island's capital, **Samothraki town,** is called the Chora by the islanders. It lies high above the port, on the lower slopes of Mount Fengari, its houses stacked in the form of an ampitheatre. These houses are rectangular, whitewashed, with windows and doors in bright greens and blues. Roofs are of round red tile, invariably weighted down with stones in the traditional Thracian manner. The narrow streets were never intended for motor traffic, although a relief road giving access to the Alonia road has been improvised. The Chora is a picturesque place to visit. Somehow it seems detached from the life of the rest of the island, if not from the twentieth century also. The only bank in the island is discreetly situated here. But there are no hotels. The Chora seems to prefer to welcome its visitors for the day only, though perhaps this might change.

**Alonia** is said to be the second town of the island, although the port has probably overtaken it. It is a cool green place, set in a well-watered valley. Its activities are purely agricultural, and of little interest to the tourist. The rapidly developing **Kamariotisa** has rather outgrown its simple framework. In addition to its transport function, it likes to think of itself as a bathing resort, as can be seen by a row of changing cubicles and a fresh-water shower. There are a number of small shops, cafés and restaurants, and on the outskirts a small modern hotel. The port is small, but well sheltered. Considerable construction work is in progress along the waterfront, which should lead to a more harmonious appearance.

More changing cubicles proclaim that **Paleopolis** too has pretensions as a bathing resort. Its museum and site are indeed the magnet for the culturally inclined. But shorn of these, the place is little more than a few isolated restaurants. **Therma** is a genuine small holiday resort, set amid the ample shade of many mature trees. At the entrance to the village, where the bus stops, is the Loutra, a tiny hot-water bathing establishment where the waters are said to be effective against arthritis. Outside, several small hot-water springs flow throughout the year. Fortunately — but a short distance away — there are a number of cold-water springs to serve the village. There are several small lodging houses and rooms to rent, a number of cafés and restaurants, and further buildings under construction. A dusty walk of 500m leads to the beach with cubicles and shower.

In the south, **Profitis Ilias** and **Xiropotamos** are small villages on the slopes of the mountain, at points where there is ample water. Profitis Ilias is most pleasant, with shady trees and trickling water. In the middle of the village there is an attractive group of tavernas, especially popular on a hot summer evening. It also enjoys a superb view, best seen from the cemetery, to Lemnos and the Turkish mainland. Below, **Lacoma** is of less interest. The remaining settlements are very small.

## Accommodation

### Hotels in Samothraki

| Class | Name | | Rooms | Tel. (code 0551) |
|---|---|---|---|---|
| **At Kamariotisa** | | | | |
| B | Aeolos | | 56 | (NYK) |
| C | Niki Beach | | 38 | 41561 |
| **At Paleopolis** | | | | |
| B | Xenia | Paleopolis | 7 | 41230 |
| **At Loutra** | | | | |
| B | Kaviros | | 28 | 41577 |

and two other lower category hotels.

**Private accommodation** Rooms can be rented in the larger villages already mentioned.

## Camping

The island has no organised campsite, although an unofficial one is believed to have opened recently near Therma. Most of the island is unpropitious for camping, although tents are found pitched in surprising places. Mostly there is little shade, and access to possible sites can be difficult except on foot or motorbike. The best area is in the north east, beginning soon after Paleopolis. Here there are groves of mature plane trees, often extending down to the beach. Every village has communal water, and there are some taps elsewhere. Camping gas exchange bottles will not be found.

## Beaches

Most of the island beaches are of similar character, comprising large or medium irregularly shaped stones and very little sand. The water usually shelves gradually, and some shallows abound with small boulders. The three bathing establishments on the north coast are not much different. Their condition is tidier, there are changing cubicles and a shower, and refreshments are available. The sea itself is clear and transparent.

The north coast is accessible for most of its length. In summer the prevailing wind gusts down the mountainside and the sea often seems rather rough. Access to the south coast is more difficult except in the extreme west. A motor track leads south from Lacoma, where a typical beach has the benefit of an isolated taverna, a water tap, and a few small fishing boats. The waters in the south are usually calmer.

Exceptionally, there is the small isolated sandy beach of **Pahia Amos**. It is mentioned only for completeness, since it is extremely difficult to get to. Beyond Lacoma, a very rough motor track can be followed to its end at the church of Panagia Kremniotisa. A track can then be followed parallel to the river bed. At some stage, depending on the cross country capability of your vehicle, it will be necessary to get out and walk.

## Agriculture

The rolling cornfields of the extreme west, dotted with occasional trees, present an unusual sight. More conventional are the extensive olive plantations of the south coast.

The predominant tree is the plane which, provided water is available, propagates itself with astonishing felicity. In contrast to Thassos and the Sporades, pine trees are seldom seen.

## Historical background

From the beginning, Samothraki had some importance because of its position near the entrance to the Dardanelles. From the top of Mount Fengari, Poseidon the Sea God is said to have followed the progress of the Trojan War. On a clear day, he would have had an excellent view. At one stage the island possessed a considerable population, a large fleet, and even founded a colony at present-day Alexandroupolis. From time to time new groups of settlers came to the island — Phoenicians, Thracians, and Aeolians from Lesbos. Out of this melting pot a religious cult emerged, based on the usual male and female fertility symbols. Little is precisely known of its origins, but it is clear that its gods, the Cabeiri — collectively known as the Great Gods — were found to be extraordinarily powerful. The Greeks, however argumentative in politics, were surprisingly tolerant in religious matters. Local gods with a proven track record could easily be given honorary membership of the Pantheon. Thus Axierus was considered a manifestation of Demeter, and Kadmilos of Hermes. At the annual religious celebrations, pilgrims came eventually from all over the Mediterranean world. The privileged could be invited for initiation into the sacred rites. Such initiations would result in favours in return, presents, donations, even the endowment of new buildings. Philip II of Macedon, father of Alexander the Great, was a notable initiate. Only marginally a Greek himself, he was happy to identify himself with this originally non-Greek religion.

*Remains of a temple. From the site of the Heiron at Paleopolis, there is a magnificent view across the blue Aegean to the mainland. This complex is relatively little visited, and devotees can roam at will among the ancient stones, absorbing the unique atmosphere of the Sanctuary of the Great Gods.*

Later the Romans, who liked to think of themselves as successors of Troy, also lent the cult their support. The end came in the 6th century AD, when the entire religious complex was destroyed by earthquake.

Thereafter the story is the familiar one of decline under the Byzantines and Turks. There was brief stability under the Genoese. Later the population reduced greatly, often to provide new settlers to shore up outlying parts of the empire.

The site of the Sanctuary of the Great Gods began to be explored by French archeologists in the 1860s. Their leader, M.Champoiseau, for many years the French consul in Istanbul, was lucky enough to discover the famous **Nike,** a headless statue also known as the Winged Victory of Samothrace. It is believed to have been a gift from Demetrius Poliorcetes, King of Macedon, in thanks for his naval victory over Ptolemy II in 305 BC. The French took it to the Louvre, where it now stands imposingly at the head of the main entrance staircase. More recent excavations have been under American auspices. As a result, there is now an excellent small museum, with inscriptions in Greek and English. This lies a short distance to the south of the coast road at **Paleopolis.** The vehicle entrance leads to a parking space at the rear of the museum. The original approach 200m further east, is a mule track which leads past the museum entrance, before continuing up to the Chora.

A visit to the Sanctuary is best started in the Museum. Exhibits include a fine reproduction of the Nike (not surprisingly donated by the French Government). Also one can buy very cheaply an excellent little pamphlet in English, containing a sketch plan of the site, and a brief description of each building. The site itself lies a few hundred metres south east of the museum, its buildings grouped at the bottom of a valley. On the hill beyond, it is possible to see some remaining fortified walls of the original city. No buildings from this remain, but the conspicuous ruin of a fifteenth century Genoese castle stands within the city walls. The ancient harbour was on the point of land below this castle. The castle can very easily be seen from the approaching ferry, as also can the (re-erected) columns of the Heiron — the building in which the most exclusive initiations took place. The whole site is best viewed from the low hill on which stands the Stoa — the ancient hostel in which pilgrims to the sanctuary were housed.

Both museum and site are open 7 days a week, from 0900-1900. On Sundays, the hours are shorter — 1000-1630 — but admission is free. For the rest of the week, 35dr each are charged for entrance to the museum and the site.

In remoter parts of Samothraki, a few old men can be seen wearing **traditional costume** as a matter of course. The shirt has very wide sleeves. Below, knee length baggy trousers are supported by a cummerbund. On the feet leather sandals are worn over short black stockings.

# Walks and excursions

Most visitors will want to visit the archeological site at **Paleopolis,** and to take a stroll through the **Chora.** Both of these can conveniently be reached by public buses.

Thereafter, the possibilities are more limited. The bus can be taken to **Therma** or **Lacoma,** and walks can be made in an easterly direction through little visited countryside. The western tip of the island can easily be explored from the port (about one hour). There is a fresh water lagoon, where a modest amount of fish farming takes place. The reeds on its bank provide an interesting habitat for birds.

The mountain behind the Chora can be climbed without great difficulty (it is said in about four hours). This is some 200m below the highest peak. Nevertheless the view is spectacular on a clear day.

There are not yet any regular boat trips, although sufficient tourists now come to the island for a limited programme to be profitable. Meanwhile, a caique could be chartered. A visit to the sandy beach at **Pahia Amos** would be enjoyable. About 6kms further east there is a waterfall at **Kremasta Nera.** Indeed a boat trip round the whole island would be an experience, especially for the grandeur of the south east, where the mountains tumble down steeply into the sea.

Samothraki today has no obvious basis for prosperity. The proportion of fertile land is small. Tourism is not a major industry. There are no factories, nor mines. There is some fishing but little forestry.

Nevertheless, there are signs of material prosperity, exceeding that of other better-endowed islands, to be seen all around. In fields and villages lie many expensive agricultural machines, such as combine harvesters and powerful tractors. The roads are full of pick-ups and motor cars, often new and owned by local people. Many new buildings are being constructed. The source of this prosperity is something of a mystery — unless it be that the Great Gods continue to look after their own!

*Samothraki town: some of the houses, stacked in an amphitheatre on a lower slop of Mount Fengari. Note the roofs, weighed down with rows of stones in the Thracian style. When this photo was taken, the road to Alonia was being rebuilt below the tree-line.*

**IMPORT AND EXPORT OF ANTIQUES**

Antiquities may be imported into Greece free of duty, provided they are declared on entry by the owner; failing this, they will be regarded as having been acquired in Greece and their re-export will be banned. Antiquities imported into Greece and declared at Customs may be re-exported free of any other formality.

Antiquities may be taken out of the country only on a special permit issued by the Ministry of Culture and Science. The Greek state has the right to prohibit the export of any one antique object, in which case, if the interested party seeks its exportation the state is under obligation to purchase the antique in question for half the price declared by the exporter. Any attempt to carry out of the country illegally items of antique value is liable to prosecution. Moreover, any person found guilty of assisting in the illegal export of any antique object is considered an accomplice and is liable to prosecution.

**PURCHASE AND EXPORT OF COPIES OF ANTIQUITIES**

There is a permanent exhibition of frescoes, plaster casts and copies of various masterpieces found in museums all over Greece, in the National Archaeological Museum of Athens. The objects on display are for sale and can be exported without any formality.

*The accessibility of Greece's rich heritage of antiquities has always proved tempting to collectors and souvenir hunters. The Greek state now has strict controls to prevent antique works being taken out of the country illegally and penalties for infringement are severe.*

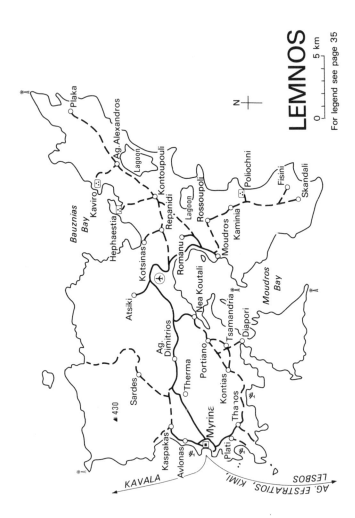

# LEMNOS

0 _____ 5 km

For legend see page 35

TWELVE

# Lemnos

*Population: 15,721*      *Highest point: 430m*
*Area: 476 sq. kms*      *Hotel beds: about 650*

First impressions of Lemnos (Limnos) are not auspicious. The rolling hillsides seem totally devoid of trees, or even scrub, scorched in summer to a dull dusty brown. And from the moment of stepping ashore from ship or aircraft, it becomes obvious that Lemnos is a garrison island.

Lemnos is indeed most strategically placed, directly opposite the entrance to the Dardanelles. That vital sea lane gives access to the Mediterranean from the Black Sea ports belonging to both Turkey and Russia. During the First World War, the island was the major operating base for the Allied assault on Gallipoli. It can hardly be a secret that the installations built then, and others since, continue in use today. The tourist comes across them, and their occupants on manoeuvre, all over the island. The young men are friendly enough, to be sure. But enjoyment of photography can be marred by fear of pointing camera or binoculars in some forbidden direction. Best to take care!

The island is of volcanic origin, formed of lava and sandstone. The great indentations of Moudros Bay, together with a smaller bay on the north coast, nearly succeed in cutting it in two. In the vicinity of this isthmus there are large expanses of flat fertile land. Hills rise towards all four corners, most steeply towards the north west, which is particularly barren and inaccessible.

The summer climate of the island seems especially invigorating. Dry cooling winds blow steadily during the day, and there are no mountains, as on Samothraki, high enough to cause gusting. Often there are faint traces of sulphur on the air, which may well be beneficial to breathing. Sulphur also seems to soften the skin.

Lemnos has a reputation for scarcity of water, which today seems unjustified though no doubt the situation sometimes causes headaches for the water authorities. In summer pressure may be reduced but it's rare for the taps to run dry.

The island is too remote, and too devoid of obvious attractions, to be visited by many tourists. Many of those who come have some family connection with the island. A select few are drawn by the luxury of the Akti Myrina development (see Accommodation below); others come just to get away from mass tourism.

## Arrival by air

Lemnos has a large airport, situated near the head of Moudros Bay. This serves both civil and military purposes, and its runway is more than adequate for the Boeing 737s and SH3s of Olympic Airways. There are up to three daily flights from Athens, one daily from Thessaloniki, and up to four flights a week from Lesbos. Although the former is further, its air fare is cheaper. Indeed a flight from Athens costs little more than a combined journey by sea and overland. Flying time from Athens is 45 mins by 737, and 70 mins from Thessaloniki. Flights become fully booked during periods of military leave, so early reservation is advisable. Buses between Myrina and the airport (22kms) run as necessary.

## Arrival by sea

The nearest mainland port is Kavala, giving a journey time between 5 and 6 hours to the capital Myrina. Three companies compete on the route.

Loucas Nomicos schedules vary considerably with season. Their regular ferry, the 'Skopelos', usually calls twice in each direction on a route between Kavalla and Agios Konstandinos (11½ hrs). Variations include a return to Lesbos (6 hrs), and — especially in winter — the substitution of Kimi for Agios Konstandinos. In summer another ferry, probably the 'Aegeus', should call weekly, so giving the slight chance of a direct connection with one of the North Sporades.

The Maritime Company of Lesbos is a major Aegean shipping company, operating three large car ferries. 'Alceos' is the smallest of their fleet, but by far the largest ferry to operate out of Kavala.

Officers and sailors are immaculately uniformed, and the ship is kept as clean as the habits of some passengers permit. From Lemnos, a weekly service continues all the year round to Lesbos (6hrs), and eventually Piraeus (19hrs).

Finally there is an elderly car-ferry called 'Kyklades', which wanders on a weekly schedule around the outer reaches of the Aegean, between Piraeus and Kavala. Agapitos Lines is the operator. Ports of call vary, but currently include Lemnos, Lesbos, Chios, Samos, Ikara, Leros, Kalymos, Rhodes, and Crete. Timings are uncertain, so it is essential to contact the agent the previous day.

It will be seen that all operators have, to some extent, long chain schedules, from which three undesirable consequences arise. Thus sailings and arrivals may be at inconvenient times, even during the middle of the night. Delays, once incurred, may be difficult to make up. And at the height of the season, Lemnos as the first island after the mainland port can be easier to get to than to get away from! This is because the ship always starts from the mainland with complete capacity, but in the other direction it may arrive already full, and offload only a handful of vehicles and passengers. On such occasions it may be easier to obtain a passage, albeit expensively, to a more distant mainland port.

Fares are not uniform. Currently 'Alceos' — with a larger capacity to fill — and 'Kyklades' — handicapped by uncertain timings — seem cheaper.

## Road system

A broad tarmac road joins Myrina to Moudros, passing the airport on the way. Short tarmac sections connect Atsiki, Romanu and Nea Koutali to this road. Unsurfaced secondary roads continue to all the villages. These are kept in fairly good condition, being regularly used by buses or military vehicles. Except in the north west, most parts of the island, both inland and on the coast, are accessible to ordinary motor vehicles.

**Buses** At first sight the island enjoys a good network of public bus services, which connect all the larger villages to Myrina. In fact frequency of service is rather low, averaging only twice daily. And since it is intended to meet the needs of the villages, the bus usually starts from there, which is inconvenient for the tourist. In the case of Plaka and Skandali, each with a single daily service, an overnight stay would be unavoidable. (But see also Excursions.)

**Taxis** No doubt arising from the restricted policy of the bus company, the island enjoys an unusually large number of taxis.
**Petrol** There are two stations for petrol and diesel fuel in Myrina, and one each in Moudros, and on the Myrina side of the airport.

# Centres of population

### Myrina

The capital of Lemnos is **Myrina** (Mirina, Kastron), indisputably a town. Although in turn administered from Lesbos, there are offices of civil administration, even a Bishop, as well as a number of dignified buildings of nineteenth century origin. The town — dominated by its Kastro, a steep, rocky, volcanic hill — sprawls around two bays on either side of the Kastro, with the port to the south and the main residential area inland and to the north. The port is well sheltered but congested. In addition to ferries, a succession of small freighters unload their cargo into lorries. The people of Myrina, sitting at innumerable tables outside cafés, seem quite unperturbed by the noise and confusion. More picturesquely, an inner harbour shelters caiques. The post office is in the port area.

The main shopping street, narrow but mercifully almost free of motor traffic, runs north from opposite the caique harbour. Towards its far end is the bus station. Several tourist agencies are situated in the main street, rather than the port. A rather fragmentary ring road runs round the back of the town, connecting the three roads emanating from the capital with the approach road to the port. The northern promenade, being unsuitable for use by through traffic, is pleasantly quiet.

Myrina has all the facilities expected of the capital of a substantial Greek island. Cars, motorbikes and bicycles can be hired: prices seem rather expensive, even compared to the mainland, but then the hiring season is short. There is a sizeable hospital. The wife of one of its consultants runs what is by far the best handicrafts shop in the main street (Hephaistia Antiques).

The museum, which contains finds from local sites, is situated on the North Promenade. At the time of writing, it was closed for restoration. The capital is also where you will find the island's two or three banks. Myrina is a designated entry port for yachts arriving in Greek waters.

## Moudros

**Moudros** is the second town of the island. It lies scattered untidily around a low hill, on which stands a large and conspicuous church. Without its garrison function Moudros would have withered to very little, although the recent completion of a new hotel now offers the prospect of some tourist infusion. There are a few fishing boats, and a single stone pier serves to unload two or three small freighters away from the congestion of Myrina. Otherwise, little has been made of what could have been an attractive waterfront. There is a Post Office, and on the road towards Rossoupoli, a cemetery of the Imperial War Graves Commission. (On the opposite side of the bay, especially near Portiano, other World War One remains may be discovered.)

## Other villages

The island has many villages, large and small. Almost without exception their function is agricultural, and their situation chosen for cultivating a nearby area of fertile land. Thus for protection, and also to free good land for cropping, many villages were constructed on rocky hillsides, even inside extinct craters.

The village way of life continues today with few changes from the past. This life centres on the village open space, and the cafés which invariably surround it. During the day, the village elders sit around, and decide all those small matters needing communal consensus, and on summer evenings tables spill out almost filling the space completely. On feast days and at weddings, great celebrations take place in all villages. But if a village is fortunate enough to have a wide open space, and traffic is slight or can be diverted, then on most summer weekends the eating and drinking will be supplemented by music and dancing. Once a village has a reputation for this, even townspeople will motor out to join in the fun. At present **Tsimandria** is popular, with the additional attraction of an outstanding fish restaurant. Evening visits to **Agios Dimitrios, Nea Koutali** or **Sardes** might also be rewarding, but it would be better to enquire first.

In other respects, it cannot be said that any village is so exceptional as to demand a visit. But opportunities to see some of them will arise in the course of visits to beaches, archeological sites, and other excursions. The motorists is warned that, away from the main roads, most of the villages have exceptionally narrow and twisting main streets, and that the way through is seldom obvious!

## Accommodation

### Hotels in Lemnos

| Class | Name | | Rooms | Tel. (code 0276) |
|-------|------|---|-------|------------------|
| **At Myrina Beach** | | | | |
| Luxe | Akti Myrina | (Bungalows) | 125 | 22681 |
| **At Myrina** | | | | |
| A | Astron | (Apartments) | 12 | 24392 |
| B | Castro Beach | | 74 | 22772 |
| B | Nefeli | (Apartments) | 12 | 23415 |
| C | Lemnos | | 29 | 22153 |
| C | Sevdalis | | 36 | 22691 |
| C | Afroditi | (Apartments) | 12 | 23489 |
| **At Moudros** | | | | |
| B | To Kyma | | 22 | 71333 |

and two other lower category hotels.

Almost all the hotels are in Myrina. There is also one in Moudros, and a small one in Agios Dimitrios.

On the northern outskirts of Myrina is situated one of the only two De-Luxe category hotels of any of the islands covered by this book. The Akti Myrina is known locally as Little Switzerland, not on account of any Alpine scenery, but for its Swiss financial backing, and nucleus of Swiss clientele.

The complex is exceptionally attractive, its concept often attempted, but seldom with such success. High quality individual bedroom chalets blending inconspicuously into a riot of colourful trees and shrubs, are grouped around the central facilities. The hotel has a splendid private beach, with water sports and excursions in its own caique, swimming pools, tennis courts, night club etc. There are four restaurants (some open to the general public) serving high class international menus. Naturally such lavish facilities, open for only five months of the year, are expensive: but those who can afford them will probably be well satisfied.

Rather cheaper is the modern and efficient Hotel Castro, well situated on the northern Promenade next to the Museum.

**Private accommodation** Myrina has a number of self-catering apartments for rent, often of good quality. The tourist agencies have details.

Private rooms are available in some of the villages. Enquire at the tourist agencies, or by ringing the village telephone number, or at the village Police Station.

*It's well worth walking up the steep hill to the Kastro above Myrina to see the splendid view of the town with its harbour and beaches far below. In this photo the line of concrete blocks emerging from the water represents work in progress to extend the quayside — now completed.*

## Camping

The island is quite suitable for camping, since few campers come, and are therefore well tolerated by police and local people. There are no organised campsites, but neither are No Camping signs often seen. Access to peaceful and remote spots, not too far from water and shops, is fairly easy. Away from the north west, suitable sites could be found in most parts, scarcity of shade being the most restrictive factor. Perhaps the west end of the south coast is the most favourable part — see also under Beaches below.

All towns and villages have communal water taps. There are also springs in some places, and wells in low lying areas — a bucket with rope is usually concealed nearby. Readers are reminded that water is a valuable item and these sources are often the mainstay of the population, and should never be abused.

Camping gas exchange bottles are not stocked.

## Beaches

The coastline is extensive, with many indentations, and accessible in most parts. There is therefore a wide choice of beaches, some of them very good. The better and more accessible beaches are often served by small cafés or tavernas. Myrina has sandy beaches both to the south (Turkish Beach) and to the north (Greek Beach). The latter is more spacious, with olive trees planted to give shade. Further north, a sandy beach at **Avlonas** is deserted except for the power station, and some turtles in a stream. **Kaspakas** — in Turkish times a holiday resort for important functionaries — overlooks a broad sandy bay, with more small beaches beyond.

On the north coast there are pleasant sandy beaches around **Kotsinas**, and also to the east of **Hephaestia.**

Much of the east coast is low lying. There are two salt lagoons which dry out altogether in the summer. The coastline is mostly sandy, with some enormous unbroken beaches though, unfortunately, the sand is often covered by deposits of seaweed, driven up by the prevailing wind.

**(Opposite)** *One of the 'Flying Dolphins' — hydrofoils purchased from the USSR — which now provide a fast, comfortable service between many islands. (Photo: D.F. Laoudis, Ceres Hydrofoils S.A.)*

The sheltered waters of Moudros Bay can be reached in many parts, though most of its beaches are not particularly attractive. But at **Diapori,** set near a narrow isthmus at the head of Kontias Bay, the sandy beach shelves steeply to allow excellent swimming: there is even some shade from a few olive trees fringing a taverna. Between Kontias and Plati there are a number of bays with sandy beaches, both large and small, but mostly little used. The beach at the end of the valley below **Thanos** has more shade than most.

## Agriculture and products

Trees do not grow naturally, but can be planted. If watered during the summer, and sheltered in winter, they have a fair chance of becoming established. But it's an uphill struggle: many die prematurely, and only a small proportion manage to grow perfectly upright.

Large areas of wheat occupy the lower lying fertile ground. That this is a traditional crop can be seen from the large number of windmills, standing on hillsides near the wheat-growing villages, today in various stages of dilapidation. Advantage is taken of the grain and straw to raise horses and cattle. Kontoupoli is the centre for horse breeding, and there are horse races on 23 April, St George's Day, and in October. Sesame seed is also grown, and will be found decorating most of the bread baked on the island. A small amount of good quality cotton grows round Rossoupoli.

A significant amount of wine is produced, most of it sold through local shops. Red and white are found, both quite pleasant and inexpensive, the latter having the less astringent flavour.

The product to which the tourist's attention is most drawn is honey. Its special quality lies in the thyme which grows abundantly all over the island. It is, however, more than twice as expensive as the honey of Thassos. The islanders tell you this is because it is more than twice as good. A more plausible explanation is that they have the good sense to produce no more than they can dispose of locally.

**(Opposite)** *Grave of Rupert Brooke. In this remote and isolated part, the silence is broken only by the calling of birds and the rustle of the breeze through the olive trees. The simple grave, recently renovated, is maintained by the Anglo-Hellenic Society.*

*The trellis outside this cottage in a remote part of Lemnos hangs thickly with ripe grapes, interspersed with gourds. Omar Khayyam would have been delighted to sit in its cool shade with his book of verses, beside a jug of wine and loaf of bread! Lemnos can easily provide these simple pleasures.*

Birds seem to find Lemnos to their liking. Fruit and vegetables, grown mainly for private consumption, are very much at risk. But the holidaymaker will enjoy several exotic species — Bee-eater, Roller and Hoopoe among them — which are seen in the UK only as rare summer migrants.

**Lemnian Earth** In ancient times great quantities of earth were dug up, and used as a remedy for wounds and stomach ailments. The source was near Repanidi, and effectiveness must have been due to the sulphur content — naturally this was long before the discovery of sulphonamides. The famous Greek physician Galen who lived in the second century AD, spent some time in Lemnos in an attempt to investigate its properties. In Turkish times there was even fear that the reserves might be exhausted. A decree was therefore issued limiting extraction to one wagon load each year.

**Fishing** Some fishing is carried out from Myrina and Moudros. But caiques mostly operate from various sheltered beaches, and tiny improvised harbours.

**Sponges** Nea Koutali is the base for a sponge diving industry, one of the few remaining in the Aegean. These are exported, and can also be bought relatively cheaply on the island.

# Historical background

The ancient Gods, living above Mount Olympus, would have been able to see Lemnos, low on the eastern horizon. Homer tells us that Hephaestos (Vulcan) the Fire God was once rash enough to intervene in one of the many quarrels between his parents Zeus and Hera. The outraged Zeus seized the foolish fellow, and flung him off the mountain. He fell onto Lemnos, where he was lucky enough to escape with only a broken leg.

In this part of the Aegean, it was the women of Lesbos whose reputation for unusual social practices was the better known. But the women of Lemnos also have their modest niche in history. Hephaestus was again involved. His wife was Aphrodite, Goddess of Love, whose extra-marital adventures were too much for the prudish women of Lemnos to put up with. They were unwise enough to throw her statue into the sea, whereupon the Goddess in revenge afflicted them all with terrible body odour and bad breath.

No doubt Aphrodite foresaw very well the reaction of the husbands. Before long expeditions were made to the mainland, and Thracian women were brought back and installed as concubines.

But the Lemnian women were made of stern stuff. Eventually they arranged a feast for the husbands and their girlfriends: after making them all drunk, they killed the lot, and threw their bodies into the sea.

This was one of several murky events involving Lemnos, which gave rise to the expression 'Lemnian deeds', used in classical times to denote foul, treacherous and disgraceful conduct.

The sequel is also interesting. Some years later, Jason and his Argonauts called at the island during their search for the Golden Fleece. They were lucky enough to find themselves in a sailor's paradise, inhabited only by women. Presumably the women had recovered from their afflictions, since after the sailors had left, the island was successfully repopulated.

The name Lemnos is of Phoenician origin. Archeological research indicates that it was inhabited before 3000 BC, which makes it one of the earliest settlements in the Aegean. Probably it reached its peak of prosperity about the same time as Troy — across the water on the Turkish mainland — with which there was much reciprocal trading. In those days the men of Lemnos were skilful metal workers. Before Greek speaking people arrived in the North Aegean, the natives were known as Pelasgians, with their own language. Lemnos was one of the last places where Pelasgian culture and speech survived. This probably continued until 500 BC, when Miltiades, a powerful chieftain from the mainland opposite, decided to throw in his lot with Athens. With him he also brought Lemnos and Imros (an adjoining island, now Turkish). Before long, both found themselves colonies of Athens.

Subsequent history is similar to that of nearby islands. In 1770, the Russians under Orloff attempted to take it from the Turks. Unlike the similar episode at Thassos, they were not successful. In 1912, the island was liberated by the Greek navy.

As already described, Moudros Bay was a major base for the Allied fleet at the time of the Gallipoli landings. Winston Churchill, then First Lord of the Admiralty, is said to have stayed on the island at that time.

# Walks and excursions

The island is large, and transport is needed to see much of it. Holidaymakers based near Myrina will find excursion bus tours run by the Petridou Tourist Agency more convenient than the public buses. Excursions last all day, visiting several villages and an archeological site. A long break is made at midday, stopping at some beach for a swim, with lunch available at a taverna (not included in the price). During the course of a week, there will be two or three tours, with different itineraries.

There are three archeological sites of possible tourist interest:

● **Poliochni:** A very ancient city, contemporaneous with Troy. The site stands on a low hill beside the sea, some 3kms south east of Kamina. Although signposted at Moudros and Roussopoli, there is no roadside indication when the turn to the site is reached. It is therefore wise to ask at Kamina for directions. There is little to be seen apart from the foundations of ancient houses.

● **Hephaestia:** The first Athenian city on the island. By road, approach from Kontopouli — it will be necessary to ask for help to find the right exit track. This eventually runs across a beach, and through a small group of farm buildings, before leading up the hill. The site is not up there, as might be expected. Instead, a narrow but well defined footpath leads to the left, 200m beyond the farm-houses, arriving directly at the ancient theatre. Looking back, other antiquities can be seen to the left — foundations of houses, and under a corrugated roof, the remains of a bath-house. Traces of city wall can also be found.

● **Kavirio:** Situated on a promontory opposite Hephaestia, and belonging to much the same period, it is approached from Agios Alexandros. Ruins of a sanctuary can be seen : on the beach below is a cave which probably once connected with it.

All three sites are stated to have custodians. In practice, these will probably be found to be otherwise occupied.

**Kotsinas** Today this insignificant settlement is a destination for bus excursions, which use its small taverna and isolated beach. It is difficult to believe that in mediaeval times it was the island capital. A prominent bronze statue stands outside the church, in memory of a local heroine, Maroula. When her father, the local patriot leader, was killed in battle against the Turks, Maroula bravely took his place. The battle was won, but before long Turkish domination was imposed throughout the island.

Below the church, some 60 steps cut into the rock lead down to a well containing Holy Water. A torch is necessary.

On the beach can be seen traces of walls built of very large stones, remains of the mediaeval fortress. These stones were probably taken from Hephaestia. It is quite possible to walk (less than one hour) from Kotsinas to Hephaestia, using farm tracks which run parallel with the foreshore.

**Myrina — The Kastro** This is well worth climbing, if only for the fine views over the town. The track to the main entrance starts behind the terrace belonging to a prominent café overlooking the Greek beach. The present castle walls are Byzantine, with Venetian and Genoese strengthening. Traces of much earlier walls, built of very large (cyclopian) stone, can also be seen.

**Thermal springs** There are several hot springs in the island, best seen at Plaka and Therma. The bathing establishment at Therma no longer functions.

**Monastery at Agios Sozon** In the extreme south east of the island, beyond the village of Fisini, stands the isolated monastery of Agios Sozon. Although in good repair, it is no longer used.

**Boat excursions** There are no excursions as such, apart from those organised by the Hotel Akti Myrina. But it is possible to visit Agios Efstratios for the day, by caique from Myrina (see under Agios Efstratios for details).

**Fishing** There is still good fishing to be had, although less abundantly than 20 years ago, when vast quantities of lobster and other fish were landed. Some blame poaching by fishing boats from Italy, who are alleged to use explosives and other illegal devices. Others hold responsible the American and Russian fleets. These often anchor on the shallow banks between Lemnos and the Turkish mainland, which are the fish breeding grounds.

It is not difficult to arrange a trip in a fishing caique, and possibly one could be hired for the day.

**Maps** Two competing tourist maps of Lemnos can be bought in Myrina. The one by Thomas Sfounis carries an accurate representation of the road system. The other does not.

THIRTEEN

# Agios Efstratios

*Population: 296*     *Highest point: 303m*
*Area: 43 sq. kms*

There is no tourist map of Agios Efstratios. That is not surprising, because practically no tourists come, and those that do stand little chance of becoming lost: nor is there much of interest for them to want to find. The general appearance of the island is similar to that of Lemnos, as it is also of volcanic origin. Barren rolling hills rise to nearly the same height, whilst covering a much smaller area. The rock is predominantly granite and sandstone.

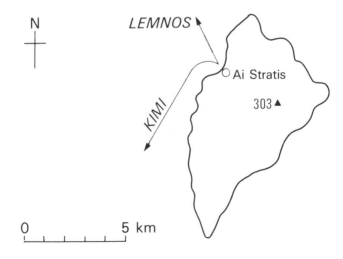

The shape of the island is triangular, with the shortest side facing Lemnos, which lies some 37 kilometres to the north. The port is situated on the west coast, where the largest valley terminates in a sandy bay. Virtually the entire population lives in the port of Agios Efstratios.

## Arrival by sea

Scheduled sea transport is a monopoly of Loucas Nomicos, whose ships visit up to three times weekly. Their main purpose is to transport the island's modest catch of fish to the mainland — the provision of which uneconomic service must be one of the conditions earning Loucas Nomicos its government subsidy! Most services start from Kavalla (7 hrs), and call at Lemnos (2 hrs) on the way. Since few goods or traffic are landed on the island, it may happen that the ferry does not call when returning in the opposite direction. For a discussion of mainland ports see under Lemnos, Arrival by sea.

Obstructions from a former jetty which was destroyed by earthquake prevent the ferry from berthing in the port. Instead, it heaves to in the bay, to be loaded and unloaded by local caique. This is quickly accomplished, a typical load being a couple of passengers and a few boxes of fish. Obviously, motor vehicles cannot land.

In fact the island is chiefly supplied by caique from Lemnos, perhaps two or three times weekly. Most of the provisions necessary for a small island community are carried this way. On the return journey, the empty bottles and boxes are perhaps supplemented by a few bales of wool. The caique takes 2½ hours each way from Myrina, with a further 3 hours for loading, unloading, and refreshing the crew. A day visit from Lemnos is therefore a possibility. Although the day and time of sailing are rather unpredictable, regular visits to the café beside the caique harbour in Myrina will eventually produce the necessary information.

## Roads

Outside the village of Agios Efstratios, there are no roads whatever. Transport has traditionally been entirely by donkey or handcart, although recently a couple of small three wheeled petrol driven trucks have made an appearance. Even the donkey tracks are infrequent. In most parts it is possible to walk across country, following faintly marked goat paths.

**(Above)** *Ag. Efstratios. The array of concrete cubes is the new village, urgently erected after the earthquake.* **(Left)** *The island's port: Ai Stratis.*

## The village

The village originally stood on the hillside beside the port, looking south across the bay. During the late 1960s it was largely destroyed by earthquake.

Afterwards an emergency village of concrete huts was laid out in a grid pattern on the floor of the valley behind the beach. A few of the derelict houses have been put in order. A number stand shattered and empty. Others have been converted to chicken houses.

Today there are several cafés, a handful of small shops, and some government offices. At the far end of the beach is a small power station. The island is connected to the telephone system. There is a refrigerated store in which fish are accumulated before despatch to the mainland.

## Accommodation

There is a small guesthouse with 9 bedrooms. Rooms could probably be found in the village (enquire at the Police Station). The island is not really suitable for camping, but it would be feasible. There is a water tap on the jetty.

## Products

The island economy depends mainly on fishing. The surrounding waters are unusually clear and unpolluted, and shoals of quite large fish can be seen swimming even in the harbour. It should be a simple matter to arrange to accompany a fishing caique, perhaps even to hire one.

Sheep and goats are kept. In the valley behind the village there are small gardens with fruit and vegetables.

Actually, conditions on the island are rather less unfavourable to trees than on Lemnos. Many species grow in the valleys. Even on the hillsides a number of oak trees have managed to propagate themselves, whilst a few have achieved spectacular size.

## Recreation

The village beach is broad and sandy, and quite satisfactory for swimming. There are small beaches nearby, not easily accessible. On the east coast there are several more beaches, but whether they are worth a trek of two hours or more in each direction is doubtful.

There are large numbers of wild rabbits in outlying parts, which are shot by the local people.

Caves are said to shelter the Mediterranean seal (*Monachus monachus*), a species which considered by some authorities to be on the verge of extinction.

## History

The history of Agios Efstratios follows closely that of Lemnos, from which it is administered. (Both form part of the prefecture of Lesbos.) In Byzantine times it was a favourite place for banishing exiles, and it has continued to be used for this purpose even into the 20th century. Indeed the number of cells in the local Police Station is far in excess of what could be required for the very peaceable population.

## Tourism

Few tourists will want to spend a holiday in Agios Efstratios, and the islanders themselves would not wish it otherwise. However an individual traveller will be welcomed hospitably, even with curiosity. The environment might just suit a keen fisherman with an overpowering need for solitude.

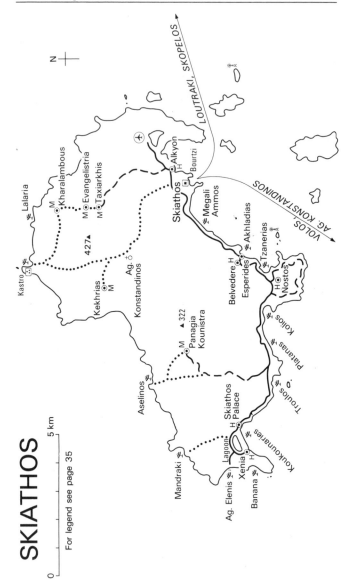

SKIATHOS

For legend see page 35

0 ————— 5 km

N

Lalaria

M Kharalambous
Evangelistria
Taxiarkhis

Kastro

427▲

Kekhrias
M

Konstandinos

Ag. ○

Alkyon
Bourtzi
Skiathos

Megali Ammos
Akhladias
Tzanerias
Belvedere
Esperides
Nostos

Kolios

Platanas

Troulos

Panagia Kounistra
M ▲322

Aselinos

Skiathos Palace

Mandraki

Lagoon
Xenia
Ag. Elenis
Banana

Koukounaries

LOUTRAKI, SKOPELOS

VOLOS, KONSTANDINOS

AG. KONSTANDINOS

FOURTEEN

# Skiathos

*Population: 4,129*      *Highest point: 427m*
*Area: 48 sq. km*       *Hotel beds: 2,779*

Skiathos welcomes with a smiling face travellers approaching from the mainland. Calm seas are probable, since the ferry passes through waters sheltered on all sides — by the Magnesian Peninsula, by Euboea, and by the other islands of the Sporades.

The approaching hills seem low, compared with the mountains of the mainland, and rise gently from west to east. Everywhere those hills are covered in vegetation. The bright green of the pines mingles with darker greens of ilexes and other evergreens, before yielding to the grey-green of the olives. Sandy beaches appear, with small boats lying securely at anchor close inshore. Clusters of white dwellings fringe the coast line, and the occasional larger bulk of an hotel can be spotted. Rounding the southernmost point of Kalamaki, the waters become calmer still, ringed by a series of small islets. The port itself finally appears, a secure anchorage in any storm. Above on two low hills stand typical whitewashed houses, each hill topped by a distinctive church.

Skiathos does well to present this smiling face, since more and more over the years it has dedicated itself to welcoming tourists, and supplying their every need. All other aspects of the island economy, even fishing, have become secondary. Should there be a conflict of interest — as for example with harvesting olives — there is no question as to which takes priority. Even the town dogs enter happily into the spirit of things. They are adept at spotting an unattached tourist, and greeting him with great affection. They follow him faithfully as he walks about, into banks and boutiques, but waiting discreetly outside food shops. Then suddenly, scenting a better prospect, they disappear as swiftly as they came.

Everything the holidaymaker might reasonably want can be bought or hired. At the peak of the season, the population of the island more than quadruples. It is not surprising that when the visitors depart, they leave behind them a trail of unused facilities. After October there is not a single hotel, restaurant or shop open outside the town, apart from a couple of tavernas fleetingly over Christmas. Even in the town, many shops and restaurants stand empty and shuttered, awaiting the return of the summer migrants. The islanders probably breathe a sigh of relief, as they enjoy a month of autumnal *dolce far niente* before the onset of winter, but already their island wears an abandoned look, bereft of its jostling throng.

# Arrival by air

The airport is only four kilometres north of Skiathos town, its runway occupying a low valley which continues the natural line of the harbour. The runway is so oriented that approach and take-off paths are entirely over the sea. It deteriorated during the 1970s, but was reopened after a major reconstruction in 1982. Olympic Airways operates up to four flights daily from Athens, using 737 and SH3 aircraft, with a flying time of 35-50 mins. Their thrice weekly service from Thessaloniki (SH3s, 50 mins) is again in operation. There are also a number of charter flights run by the package tour operators, using medium size jet aircraft.

Even on a busy day, the number of flights arriving scarcely exceeds single figures. Most people will therefore find noise levels tolerable. Buses run between terminal and town as required.

# Arrival by sea

The island enjoys a frequent ferry service operated by Loucas Nomicos which co-ordinates with services to the other Sporades islands. The major operating port is Volos, especially for freight traffic. For the convenience of foot passengers from the south, for whom there is a special connecting bus service from Athens, a fairly frequent service also operates from Agios Konstandinos. From both ports, all sailings call first at Skiathos. Most continue to Skopelos, and some also to Alonissos.

Occasional services also come up from Kimi via Alonissos and Skopelos. There is no longer a direct link between Skiros and the other Sporades. Loucas Nomicos services to Skiros are presently in abeyance, but transfer could be made at Kimi.

When volume of traffic justifies it, one or more smaller ferries may join in to serve the North Sporades. Currently G. Goutos, a company normally involved in sailings to the Cyclades from Rafina and Lavrion, may send its Papadiamantis II up to Volos. Optional calls are sometimes made to Trikeri, a tiny fishing port on the tip of the Magnesian Peninsular, which until very recently was without any motor track connection whatever. Disembarkation there would be by caique, and naturally cars could not be landed.

As mentioned in Chapter 3 the island has been served since 1985 by Flying Dolphin hydrofoils of the Ceres Company operating from Volos, Agios Konstandinos and, more recently, from Thessaloniki via Moudania (Halkadiki). An extension from Alonissos direct to Skiros is under consideration.

The slight possibility of direct car-ferry connection with Lemnos is discussed under Lemnos, Arrival by sea, and also in Chapter 3 under Island Hopping.

**To summarise:**

| From Volos | 20 - 35 sailings weekly | 3 hrs |
|---|---|---|
| | + 14 hydrofoil sailings | 1hr 20mins |
| From Agios Konstandinos | 7 - 14 sailings weekly | 3¼ hrs |
| | + 4 hydrofoil sailings | 1½ hrs |
| From Kimi | 1 - 3   sailings weekly | 5 hrs |
| From Alonissos | 7 - 14 sailings weekly | 2½ hrs |
| | + 19 hydrofoil sailings | 1½ hrs |
| From Skopelos | 20 - 30 sailings weekly | 1 hr |
| | + 19 hydrofoil sailings | ½ hr |
| From Thessaloniki | 1 + hydrofoil sailing | |
| | weekly | 3½ hrs |
| From Lemnos | (See text) | 8 hrs |

**Caiques** can sometimes be found sailing to Skiathos from small ports such as Platania, on the Magnesian Peninsula, and Vassiliki in Euboea. Sailings are unpredictable, and local enquiries must be made.

*Arrival of the ferry. M/V Skiathos approaches the jetty and a sailor throws a heaving line. Across the road, tourist agencies lie in wait: many more fringe the waterfront. On the hillside are houses with rooms for letting. There is evidence of the morning rainstorm, but the sun appeared in the afternoon.*

# Road system

A good tarmac road runs along most of the length of the south coast, linking the larger hotels and main tourist beaches with Skiathos town. In the other direction, a shorter section leads to the airport. A bypass round the back of the town permits traffic from airport to hotels to avoid the congestion of the town. A loop from the main road, tarmac for about half its length, snakes southward round the Kalamaki Peninsula, where some of the most exclusive villas have been built. Another branch, tarmac for the first kilometre, runs north to the Monastery of Kounistra.

There are a number of unsurfaced motor tracks proving of little use to tourists. The interior is criss-crossed with mule tracks of very variable condition, but most of them continue in daily use.

There has for many years been talk about extending the main road along the north coast, to form a complete ring around the island. The advantages seem dubious, since almost nobody lives in the north. And in the event the present character of that part of the island, as well as the livelihood of the fishermen who run boat trips there, would certainly be destroyed.

**Buses** Buses run between the town of Skiathos and the far end of Koukounaries Beach. Frequency varies from every half-hour in summer to every two hours in winter. The service is administered from Volos.

**Taxis** Skiathos has an abundance of taxis, usually found in the port. Some supplement the buses by cruising the length of the road. These may be stopped at will to fill any vacant seats.

**Petrol** A BP station on the outskirts of the town, on the road to Koukounaries, sells petrol and diesel fuel, with a small vehicle repair shop behind. There is also a fuel station in the port for visiting yachtsmen.

# Centres of population

The island has a single town, also called Skiathos. More than half the population live in and around it. The present town was built in the 1830s, after Greek independence, although the site of such a superb natural harbour must have been inhabited for thousands of years. The original south facing port has been outgrown, and is now used just by fishing boats.

Separating the two ports is Bourtzi, once an island, but now undeniably joined to the mainland. Its much restored Venetian fort is occupied by the primary school. Substantial extensions have been made to the new east facing port, where ferries, small freighters and visiting yachts enjoy good facilities. Along the waterfront are the usual assortment of tourist offices, bars, cafés, restaurants and small hotels. The main street runs directly inland between the two hills. Here are found the Police Station (including Tourist Police), Post Office, one of the two banks, and most of the larger shops and offices. In summer it is heavily congested.

Smaller streets seldom visited by motor vehicles run up into the interior of the town. Interesting shops, small bars and restaurants can be found, besides many a quiet corner and pleasing aspect.

There are various small settlements along the length of the main road, whose main function these days is touristic. A few shops open temporarily during the season.

# Accommodation

Nothing illustrates the explosive growth of tourism in Skiathos more than the fact that in the five years since 1983, when the first edition of this book was in preparation, the number of hotels on the island has risen from 14 to more than 60.

## Hotels in Skiathos

| Class | Name | | Rooms | Tel. |
|-------|------|---|-------|------|
| **At Skiathos Town** | | | | (code 0424) |
| B | Meltemi | (Pension) | 18 | 22493 |
| B | Akti | | 11 | 22024 |
| B | Areti | (Apartments) | 7 | (NYK) |
| C | Christina | (Apartments) | 23 | 21105 |
| C | Golden Beach | | 16 | 49325 |
| C | Kanapitsa Beach | (Apartments) | 27 | 22170 |
| C | Koukounaries | | 18 | 22048 |
| C | Margi House | (Apartments) | 12 | 49211 |
| C | Mylos | (Apartments) | 12 | 21412 |
| C | Pounda | | 34 | 21800 |
| C | Stelina | | 38 | 21900 |
| C | Toxotis | | 14 | 22111 |
| C | Vicky | (Apartments) | 11 | (NYK) |
| C | Vromolimnos | (Apartments) | 35 | 22170 |
| C | Zeus | | 15 | 49356 |

**At Koukounaries**

| | | | | |
|---|---|---|---|---|
| Luxe | Skiathos Palace | | 223 | 22242 |
| B | Mandraki | (Bungalows) | 29 | 21170 |
| B | Xenia | | 32 | 22041 |
| C | Panorama | | 12 | 49382 |

**At Ahladies**

| | | | | |
|---|---|---|---|---|
| A | Esperides | | 180 | 22245 |
| C | Belvedere | (Bungalows) | 60 | 22475 |
| C | Madoula | (Apartments) | 23 | 22581 |
| C | Souzana | (Apartments) | 8 | (NYK) |
| C | Villa Anni | (Apartments) | 8 | 21105 |
| C | Villa Kiki | (Apartments) | 20 | 22919 |
| C | Vontzos | | 18 | 22875 |

**At Tzaneria**

| | | | | |
|---|---|---|---|---|
| A | Nostos | (Bungalows) | 146 | 22420 |

**At Amoudia**

| | | | | |
|---|---|---|---|---|
| B | Alkyon | | 80 | 22981 |
| C | Princess House | (Apartments) | 8 | 22020 |

**At Plakes**

| | | | | |
|---|---|---|---|---|
| B | Orsa | (Pension) | 7 | 21975 |

**At Livadia**

| | | | | |
|---|---|---|---|---|
| C | Thymis' Home | (Pension) | 18 | 22817 |

**At Troulos**

| | | | | |
|---|---|---|---|---|
| C | Boudouriani House | (Apartments) | 10 | 22313 |
| C | Korali | (Apartments) | 50 | 49212 |
| C | Troulos Bay | | 36 | 49375 |

**At Vassilias**

| | | | | |
|---|---|---|---|---|
| C | Chryssa | (Apartments) | 9 | 22003 |
| C | Dafni | (Apartments) | 12 | 22003 |
| C | Sotiroula | (Apartments) | 6 | 22003 |

**At Ftelia**

| | | | | |
|---|---|---|---|---|
| C | Azalea | (Apartments) | 12 | 22280 |
| C | Nefi | (Apartments) | 13 | 22126 |
| C | Villa Ftelia | (Apartments) | 6 | 22606 |

**At Agia Paraskevi**

| | | | | |
|---|---|---|---|---|
| C | Villa Maria | (Apartments) | 12 | 49288 |

and 19 other lower category hotels.

**Private accommodation** Many of the villas which dot the length of the south coast can be rented. There are also a number of service apartments.

A large number of private rooms are to be let, mostly in the town. Enquire at the tourist offices, or look out for individual notices.

# Camping

Camping Skiathos (tel. (0424) 42668) is a small and very simple campsite at Kolios. Its situation beside the beach is attractive, but more trees need to be planted for shade. Some improvements, including a camp shop, are said to be projected. Water from a borehole is sometimes discoloured, and probably unfit for drinking.

There are several public taps for water in the town. Camping gas exchange bottles are stocked by several of the supermarkets.

Camping near the more popular beaches is liable to be actively discouraged by the police. There are now (1988) two other locally approved campsites on the island.

# Beaches

**Koukounaries Beach** is so exceptional that it merits special description. It has often been acclaimed, and not without justification, as the most beautiful in Greece. Many a holidaymaker will consider it close to his ideal. One thousand metres of golden sand face south, with gently shelving shallows ideal for children. The shape is like a crescent, between two rocky headlands. Behind each an hotel is discreetly perched, and so the supply of customers to generate all the beach facilities that a holidaymaker might need is thereby assured.

The beach is unusually wide, and behind it lies a broad belt of pine trees — stone pine, from which it takes its name. These give shade from the sun, and shelter from the prevailing wind.

Behind the pinegrove is a large freshwater lagoon, where the blue flash of a kingfisher in flight may be seen. At the western end it joins the sea in a narrow tongue of water, spanned by a footbridge, where a tiny harbour has evolved, now a favourite port of call for sailing flotillas. Around the lagoon a fine new golf course has recently been laid out (see below).

Koukounaries is probably unique; nor, at the height of season, will it be to the taste of all. Actually it must have been even more beautiful fifteen years ago, before the white concrete blocks of the taverna and Christo's water skiing school obtruded themselves upon the soft backdrop of the pines.

But Skiathos has, so it is claimed, as many as 70 other beaches of all types, many scarcely visited, and others accessible only by boat. Below is a summary of the principal beaches, with their more or less permanent characteristics. Starting at Skiathos town, and continuing clockwise:

**Bourtzi** At the southern tip a platform area has been constructed for swimming off the rocks.

**Megari Ammos** Sand. Convenient to the town, but overlooked by the road.

**Akhlades** Sand. Water sports and restaurants.

**Tzanerias** (Kalamaki) Sand. A cluster of beaches. Water sports and restaurants.

**Kolios** Sand. A good sheltered anchorage for boats. Campsite and restaurant.

**Platanias** Sand. Water sports and refreshments.

**Troulos** Sand. An attractively sited taverna.

**Koukounaries** as described above. All watersports, taverna and refreshments.

**Banana** (also known as Krassa). Fairly isolated. Sand. Refreshments. Naturism tolerated.

**Agia Elenis** Sand. Watersports and refreshments. Naturism tolerated.

**Mandraki** Sand. Refreshments.

**Aselinos** Sand. Isolated.

**Kastro** Sand. Isolated. (See also Historical section.)

**Lalaria** Silvery pebbles. Access only by boat. Interesting grottos nearby.

## Sports

**Tennis,** at the larger hotels.

**Golf,** at Koukounaries. A fine new course recently established privately. Much more than pitch and putt, but only the water hazards should give difficulty to the inexperienced. The scratch player is challenged by good course architecture.

**Horseriding** is bookable through tourist offices. The stables are on the outskirts of town.

**Mule excursions** enquire at tourist offices.

## Agriculture

Olive cultivation was for centuries the most important activity in Skiathos. Large areas were planted, especially in the lower areas in the east. There are still great numbers of trees in remote parts. A considerable amount of labour is involved, for bringing in pickers and pruners, and also for removing not only the crop, but also the prunings, which are invaluable for firewood. This has been achieved by mule and donkey over deteriorating tracks. The remoter areas are often now abandoned.

In recent years a number of motor tracks have been bulldozed through the more accessible parts. Nevertheless the local practice of taking a biennial harvest, resulting in a large crop of small fruit every second year, continues. By this means the cost of labour and transport is minimised relative to the overall value of the crop.

## Historical background

The historical figure most closely associated with Skiathos is the Persian king Xerxes. To this day Mandraki is also known as the port of Xerxes. Xerxes lost most of his fleet during an unusually fierce and prolonged summer gale, which drove the ships on to the rocky Magnesian coast. He therefore took the island, and set about repairing such of his ships as he could salvage. As part of the preparations for his final advance he built what is said to have been the first lighthouse in the world. It marked a rocky reef called Lefteris between Skiathos and the mainland, for he must have intended, unusually, to move his fleet by night, thus avoiding attack by the larger and more modern Athenian warships, and saving his rowers from thirst in the intense heat of the day.

In his famous Largo *(Ombra mai fu)*, Handel has this same Xerxes singing the praises of a fine plane tree, in gratitude for the cool shade cast by its branches. Skiathos has many such plane trees.
**The Kastro** Piracy was endemic in the Aegean throughout much of recorded history. The families to survive were those able to band together with others and retreat to some place sufficiently defensible from where, if necessary, they would sell their lives dearly. All the islands had such strongholds, but the measures adopted by the people of Skiathos were extraordinary. When threatened the entire

*The large caique with the eyes is named Ulysses. It belongs to an elderly Greek artist, who uses it as house, workshop and shop. At the end of Koukounaries beach, serried ranks of yachts (below) fill the entrance to the tiny harbour.*

population would leave their homes, and trek over the central mountains to the north coast, where they crossed by wooden drawbridge to this steep and rocky islet fortification. (See Excursions, below).

**Papadiamantis** Skiathos is proud of its native son, the author Alexander Papadiamantis. His stories, based on happenings in his own island, are very popular in Greece. His house in the town can be visited, and his bust occupies a prominent position at the entrance to Bourtzi. Some Greeks come to Skiathos specially to visit the places where events described in his books took place. Thus the very spot where the Turks beheaded the child who wanted to betray them, the rock where one of the heroines was drowned, the oak tree that was poisoned, and others, can be sought out.

**Local festivity** 26 July, Agia Paraskeva — Folk Dances.

# Walks and excursions

To make contact with the traditional life of the island, it is necessary to walk through the countryside, or perhaps to participate in an excursion on horseback. The selection below illustrates the possibilities; further variations could easily be devised. Where muletracks are involved, a stout pair of walking shoes is advisable. The times give the approximate duration of the excursion from Skiathos town or the starting point mentioned.

● To the northern outskirts of the town, to spot the remains of the **windmills.** (10 mins)

● From the main road behind Koukounaries — near the restaurant, signposted — to **Mandraki Beach.** A pleasant level walk along a well defined sandy path through pine woods. (20 mins)

● From the main road east of Troulos — boldly signposted — to the **Monstery of Panagia** (meaning the Virgin Mary) **Kounistra.** Refreshments at the Monastery. (45 mins) This trip could also be made by car.

● To **Aselinos Beach.** Either continue by track from Kounistra, or leave the motor road earlier as signposted, and continue direct along the valley. (1¼/1 hr)

● To **Evangelistria Monastery.** There are several possible routes for this most enjoyable excursion. The easiest to follow leaves the town ring road at a point 300m west of the turning to the airport (singposted in Greek). It continues by motor track through olive groves (this section easily negotiated by motor car) before climbing along the side of the hills. Taxiarkhis Monastery is passed — (caretaker, spring, worth seeing inside). The first sign of Evangilistria is a blue and white striped flagpole. It is said that the present Greek national flag was first hoisted on this spot in 1807 — but other places in Greece dispute this. Beyond, sheltering behind a ridge, lies the Monastery. It is the only one now occupied — one wonders for how much longer — as well as the most interesting for the non-specialist. (1½ hrs). On the far side is a spring with a picnic table. It is possible to continue from here — the track is particularly rough and narrow, but still in regular use — to the isolated **Agios Kharambous Monastery** (20 mins). From a point 300m before Kharambous (signposted in Greek) another rough track continues to **Kastro.** (45 mins).

● To **Kastro** direct. Perhaps the most rewarding excursion of all. The remoteness of the path, the wonderful views and the contrast between the north and south of the island, enhance the emotional identification which one can make with the unhappy inhabitants of earlier times, fleeing for their lives.

The first stage, to the summit near Agios Konstandinos, can be made by a variety of tracks. One has been carefully marked with frequent blobs of red paint — side tracks in regular use could easily confuse a stranger. The start is by motor track from the ring road at a shrine dated 4.9.71, and paint blobs give immediate confirmation. After 700m follow a mule track to the left — another shrine, and paint blobs immediately. Shortly after the summit a diversion could be made to Kekhrias Monastery, whose cypress trees can be seen to the left. The path continues downwards, becoming narrower but never difficult, until the Kastro is seen at the end of a promontory.

Today, some steps up the rock give access. Once there were 22 churches and some 300 houses. There remain an entrance gate, two churches, and ruins which include a turkish bath. Fine views, especially from the far lookout platform, where one is surprised to stumble across the remains of an old cannon. (2½ hrs).

● A number of boat excursions are on offer, mostly leaving from the south port. In season these run to **Skopelos** at least once daily, as well as visiting some smaller islands. Caiques to the other Sporades could probably be found. **Kastro** is most easily reached by boat, although this does not have the sense of achievement of the cross country route. The only practical way to get to **Lalaria** and some nearby beaches is by boat.

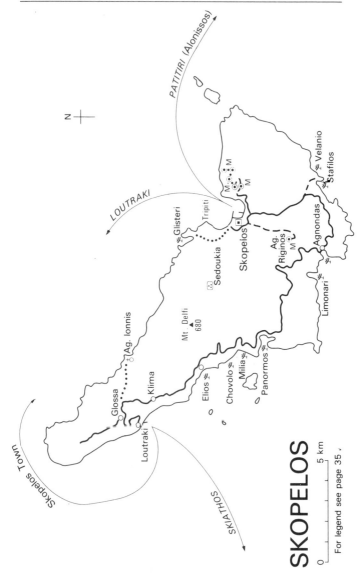

N

PATITIRI (Alonissos)

LOUTRAKI

Glisteri

Tripiti

Skopelos

Sedoukia

Ag.
Riginos

M

Agnondas

Velanio
Stafilos

M
M
M

Limonari

Ag. Ionnis

Mt. Delfi
680

Glossa

Klima

Elios

Chovolo

Milia

Panormos

Loutraki

Skopelos Town

SKIATHOS

SKOPELOS

0          5 km

For legend see page 35.

FIFTEEN

# Skopelos

*Population: 4,415*     *Highest point: 680m*
*Area: 95 sq. km*       *Hotel beds: 1249*

Skopelos is a larger island than Skiathos, but with a much smaller amount of reasonably level fertile land. The upper slopes are richly clothed with an abundance of pine trees, giving employment to some as foresters. But traditionally half the young men have had to find work outside the island.

All the Sporades have a high and deserved reputation for seamanship. The men of Skopelos are pre-eminent among them, many finding their way into the world shipping industry; currently, some five thousand ships sail under the Greek flag. Many of these exiles return eventually, perhaps bringing foreign born wives, and children who have grown up overseas. So a surprising number of inhabitants can speak another language, usually English.

Many tourists arrive in the island during the season, but provision for them does not compare with Skiathos. Moreover a number of tourist facilities are run by people from outside the island, and close immediately the main holiday season finishes.

## Arrival by sea

Skopelos has no fewer than three ports used by the ferry. Each faces a different direction, so at least one should be usable in any weather. **Loutraki,** the port of Glossa, is nearest to Skiathos. The port is well sheltered, but in a strong northerly wind there is too much fetch in the channel to permit a direct approach and usually the ferry misses out Loutraki altogether in these conditions.

**Skopelos** (town) alone among the ports of the Sporades has the temerity to face outwards, away from sheltered waters. Poseidon continues to punish it for this effrontery! The port itself is well enough sheltered, thanks to recent extensions to the breakwaters, but the long approach to the port along the north coast can cause an unacceptable amount of roll. The ferries are necessarily shallow draughted and, as is usual in the Aegean, without stabilisers. Apart from the discomfort this causes to the passengers, there is a risk of vehicles on the car deck breaking adrift. Under such conditions, the ferry uses instead the reserve port of **Agnontas.** This is a narrow rocky inlet, but with deep water, and a new quay built out on one side.

Whether the ferry berths at Loutraki or Agnontas, a bus should meet it, and take foot passengers to Skopelos. Adjustments to ticket prices are not made when the service is affected by bad weather. But normally the ferry calls first at Loutraki, and then proceeds clockwise to Skopelos.

To summarise, then (with times from Skopelos or Loutraki, whichever is nearer):

| | | |
|---|---|---|
| From Volos | 20 - 30 sailings weekly | 4 hrs |
| | + 14 hydrofoil sailings | 1½ hrs |
| From Ag. Konstandinos | 5 - 10 sailings weekly | 4 hrs |
| | + 4 hydrofoil sailings | 1¾ hrs |
| From Kimi | 1 - 3  sailings weekly | 3½ hrs |
| From Skiathos | 20 - 30 sailings weekly | 1  hr |
| | + 19 hydrofoil sailings | ½ hr |
| From Alonissos | 7 sailings weekly | ½ hr |
| | + 19 hydrofoil sailings | ¼ hr |

Since a quick way of reaching Skopelos (and Alonissos) is to take the flight to Skiathos airport, followed by a short ferry trip, the arrival information in the chapter on Skiathos is also relevant here.

## Road system

Thirty-two kilometres of good tarmac road connect Glossa and Skopelos town. It passes through spectacular scenery, with many climbs and descents. From Glossa a new road winds leisurely down to the port of Loutraki — the locals prefer to use the old donkey track. Another spur leads north for 4kms to a small military installation, which looks after the beacon used by aircraft flying into Skiathos airport opposite. There is a tarmac ring road round the back of Skopelos town, and a narrow section also winds behind the town beach.

**Buses** run from Skopelos to Glossa, and continue to Loutraki, three times daily. There are three **taxis** on the island. There are two **petrol stations** on the outskirts of Skopelos town, which also supply diesel. Surprisingly, there is none elsewhere, not even at Glossa. The locals and visiting yachtsmen can arrange to have fuel delivered in mini-road tankers.

# Centres of population

**Skopelos** town is called, locally, the Khora and is a town of some character. A broad treelined promenade runs the length of the waterfront; houses rise steeply into the hills behind, forming the shape of a triple pointed crown. The streets are narrow and twisting, though whether for shade or shelter from the wind one cannot be sure. House styles differ, but there is free use of balconies in the Venetian manner — originally in wood, later wrought iron, and nowadays sadly in concrete.

Earlier photos taken from above show a pleasing uniformity of grey-green slate roofing, but following earthquakes in the sixties, cheaper and more reliable red clay tiles made an appearance on about half the roofs of the town. Today it seems that only government buildings can afford to roof in the traditional manner. Remains of the Venetian Kastro stand on a prominent eminence, overlooking the bay. Many of its stone blocks have unfortunately been re-used elsewhere. A cascade of attractive churches runs down to the harbour, including the ninth century Agios Athanassios. Elsewhere the church of Zoodohos Pigi contains an ikon, probably fourth century, but believed by some to be from the prolific hand of St. Luke himself. Everywhere indeed there are churches, many of them tiny, and some looking like the annex to an adjoining house. Great skill is shown in many minute gardens.

Other facilities are as can be expected of a small island capital. Cars, motorbikes and bicycles can be hired. There are plans to construct a yacht marina at the north end of the harbour.

**Glossa** and its surrounding villages have nearly as many inhabitants as the Khora. It sits high on a hill overlooking the Skiathos channel, its houses tumbling down towards the sea. It is more open and more spacious than the Khora, and more countrified, with chickens scratching charmingly in the cobbled pathways. Some older houses have managed to escape earthquake damage. There are banking facilities and a chemist, and a surprisingly good disco on the outskirts.

# Accommodation

## Hotels in Skopelos

| Class | Name | | Rooms | Tel. (code 0424) |
|---|---|---|---|---|
| A | Andromachi | (Pension) | 7 | 22940 |
| A | Archontiko | (Pension) | 10 | 22049 |
| A | Kyr-Sotos | (Pension) | 12 | 22549 |
| A | Skopelos Village | (Apartments) | 25 | 22517 |
| B | Aegeon | (Pension) | 9 | 22619 |
| B | Amalia | | 50 | 22688 |
| B | Elli | (Pension) | 20 | 22943 |
| B | Mon Repos | (Pension) | 15 | 22356 |
| B | Peparithos | (Pension) | 10 | 22523 |
| B | Regina | (Pension) | 11 | 22138 |
| B | Xenia | (Pension) | 4 | 22232 |
| C | Aeolos | | 41 | 22233 |
| C | Agnanti | | 12 | 22722 |
| C | Denise | | 22 | 22678 |
| C | Adonis (ex America) | | 9 | 22231 |

**At Glossa**

| | | | | |
|---|---|---|---|---|
| C | Avra | | 28 | 33550 |

**At Panormos**

| | | | | |
|---|---|---|---|---|
| B | Panormos Beach | (Pension) | 30 | 22711 |

**At Livadi**

| | | | | |
|---|---|---|---|---|
| B | Prince Stafylos | | 49 | 22775 |
| C | Sporades | (Apartments) | 20 | 22146 |

**At Stafilos**

| | | | | |
|---|---|---|---|---|
| B | Rigas | (Pension) | 38 | 22618 |

**At Gefiraki**

| | | | | |
|---|---|---|---|---|
| C | Angelikis | (Apartments) | 17 | 22290 |

**At Eleftherotria**

| | | | | |
|---|---|---|---|---|
| C | Captain | | 17 | 22110 |

**At N. Klima**

| | | | | |
|---|---|---|---|---|
| C | Delphi | (Apartments) | 18 | 33301 |

and 15 other lower category hotels.

**Private accommodation** There is a smaller proportion of private accommodation for rent than in the other Sporades. But service apartments and private rooms are to be had, mostly in the Khora or near Glossa.

This fine house on Skopelos is typical of an earlier building tradition. The upper storey projects on supported wooden beams, giving more shade for the street below and extra space for the first floor.

## Camping

Most campers gravitate to the Panormos Bay area. There is at present no official campsite, but it is hoped regularise the situation by opening one between road and beach, beside the existing taverna. Stafilos Bay is also suitable for camping (see below.)

Camping gas exchange bottles can occasionally be found in the Khora. There are a few communal water taps.

## Beaches

The north east coast is rugged and inhospitable, and its few small coves are difficult to approach. Larger beaches only exist near the broad bay containing the Khora. The first section of the sandy town beach is not unattractive, though probably at risk from pollution during the summer. A safer bet is a shingly beach on the other side near Agios Konstantinos, with restaurant. Best of all, at a distance of 3kms, is the secluded shingly beach at **Glisteri,** approached by track through tranquil olive groves.

The south west beaches are all a mixture of fine shingle and sand. At **Loutraki** the shoreline is fringed with fine plane trees, with a small hotel, shops and cafés behind. A number of fishing boats use the beach, but there is plenty of room for swimming too. **Elios** has a long beach, where a number of concrete houses have been built. These look like a holiday complex, but are in fact emergency accommodation for those whose homes were damaged by earthquake.

**Milia** is a fine beach, isolated and without facilities, but probably the best on the island. A new approach track has been built, which also serves to reach the adjoining **Chovolo.**

**Panormos** is a large sheltered bay, full of campers in summer. At its southern end a long narrow inlet gives superb shelter for yachts and caiques. **Agnontas** has a small beach, beside the taverna. In summer fishing boats take bathers to the nearby cove at **Limonari.** This charming beach is virtually inaccessible by land, although a new motor track leading in that direction is half complete.

**Stafilos Bay** is pleasant enough, but better still is the adjoining **Velanio.** This is completely secluded behind steeply sloping cliffs. Campers wishing to disport themselves in the nude find it very attractive.

*The ferry approaches Skopelos. Now that the breakwater has been extended, the ferry can be scheduled to spend the night in port in perfect safety, before returning to Volos next morning. In the foreground is one of a cascade of churches which runs down from the Kastro towards the harbour.*

## Agriculture and products

Tree crops have usually been found most suitable for the land which is cultivated. Among them the olive, so undemanding in its requirements, takes pride of place. Nowadays it is as important for its prunings, which are carefully gathered for firewood, as for the fruit: this is labour intensive to harvest, and in any case commands a low price. Interspersed with the olives are many plum trees, as well as almonds, quinces and other fruit trees. The island continues to have a high reputation for prunes — in which form the plums emerge from the drying ovens — but the industry is in decline. Most trees are too elderly to ensure reliable cropping, and harvesting and drying conflict with the peak of tourism.

Quinces are made into jam, and are also bottled. To be given a small dish containing a few quince slices is a compliment, expressing the hope that the recipient will return to the island.

Near Glossa, in the small and undistinguished village of Klima, the roadside is usually littered with a number of old oil drums, containing a dirty wax-like substance, which is in fact pine resin. It is tapped from the trees in much the same way as latex is taken from rubber trees. Collection is centralised at Klima, before being sent to the mainland for processing. Most of it ends up as turpentine. But one would like to think that some of it finds a more noble use as flavouring for 'retsina'!

Not long ago vines were a significant crop, and wine was exported. Recently disease struck, leaving only an occasional isolated vineyard. But fine individual plants shade many a private garden. Apparently some wine is made direct from pine resin, but the result must be very much an acquired taste!

Much of the island's rock can easily be split, so it is useful building material. Dry stone walling is found everywhere. There are also some good examples of stone facing. Most highly regarded of all are the thin grey green slates known as 'plaka' traditionally used for roofing.

## Historical background

The first settlers are believed to have come from Crete. Their legendary leader Stafilos was thought to have been the son of Ariadne, daughter of the Cretan King Minos. His father was the equally legendary Prince Theseus, who happened to be in Crete at the time on a mission to slay the Minotaur. Ariadne helped him succeed, and they then eloped together, before Theseus abandoned her on the island of Naxos, during his return journey to Athens. No doubt still preoccupied with recent events, he forgot to change the colour of his sails, a signal previously agreed with his father. White was for success, but black for death. The old man saw the black sails, and in his grief, took his own life. So Theseus became King of Athens, and is credited with starting that city state on its path towards greatness and expansion.

Local tradition always held that Stafilos died and was buried at the bay that bears his name. Three millennia later, in 1927, a royal grave was discovered whose rich remains were taken to the museum in Volos. Astonishingly, the archeologists were able to pronounce that the grave was indeed that of Stafilos. Which goes to show how remarkable can be the continuity of legend, handed down by word of mouth over thousands of years (or if you prefer, the wish fulfilment complex of the archeologist!)

Homer, who told us about Theseus, called the island Peparithos. Athens and Sparta disputed its ownership. Rome wanted it enough to invade it several times. After the Fourth Crusade it came under the ownership of the Franks. They licensed it to the Venetians, who used it as a fortified trading post. In 1538 it was taken by Barbarossa — Turkish admiral or pirate according to your historical viewpoint — who massacred the entire population. For many years it remained completely deserted. Perhaps these perils and uncertainties were responsible for the large number of churches. New ones continue to be built.

**Local festivities** 6 August — Metamorphosis (Transfiguration); 25 February — Agios Riginou.

# Walks and excursions

High hills rise away from the Khora, indented by valleys. Many a monastery and church was built on these slopes. No doubt it was because of the shortage of young men that most were used as nunneries. Two of them — Evangilistria and Prodomos — continue to function as such.

● A fine group of monasteries is situated to the north east. A new motor track makes the beginning of the exploration much easier. Very conspicuous, and enjoying a superb view of the town, is

**Evangilistria.** It houses a dozen nuns, and is regularly open for visiting both in the morning and evening. One of its two tiny churches is particularly attractive. Woven and embroidered goods are sometimes on sale, although it is rumoured that fewer are made by the nuns than by occupants of the local prison.

On the opposite side of the same valley, but more easily reached from its own motor track, is the disused monastery of **Metamorphosis.** A monk is sometimes on hand to open it to visitors (the notice proclaiming regular visiting hours no longer seems to be correct). At the beginning of August it becomes the focus for the island's most important festival.

Over the top of the hill, looking out from a craggy height towards Alonissos, are three more monasteries, of which **Prodromos** is still used by nuns. The circuit can be completed, following the rough mule tracks which link all five monasteries. (About 3 hrs plus viewing time).

● To the south of the Khora, another motortrack leads after more than 4kms to the disused monastery of **Agios Riginou.** The name refers to an early bishop, martyr, and subsequently Patron Saint of the island. Near the beginning of this track, only 100m from the ring road, there is an interesting castle-like building, built when memories of pirates were still fresh, as the fortified **Monastery of Episcopi.**

● Some 6kms north west of the town, on the slopes of Mount Delphi, are some ancient rock graves called **Sedoukia.** A guide is advisable.

● From Glossa, the road towards the air base gives splendid views in all directions. (Photography definitely not advisable here.)

For the adventurous there is a rewarding walk by mule track to the church of **Agios Ioannis** (St. John), on the rugged north east coast. The path starts 100m up the road to the air base. The destination is first seen from the top of the penultimate ridge (shrine), together with another isolated building not far from it. This turns out to be a small church — the English part of its inscription reads 'U.S.A. 1954' — at which point the mule track is left. The final section begins on the far side of the church, and leads down to a small sandy cove. Beyond, at the top of a high rock projecting out to sea, stands the church. More than 100 steps cut into the slate lead precariously to the summit — fortunately the handrails are in good condition. Outside the church, at the very top of the rock, there is a well. Inside, a picture of St. George slaying the dragon is equally surprising (St. George being patron saint of Skiros). In summer the setting is a blue idyll of tranquillity: in winter one might be reminded of the bleak coast of North Cornwall. (1 hr).

● In good weather boats from the town ply to little coves nearby, and also visit the double entranced grotto of **Tripiti**. Fishing is said to be good in these waters.

*The houses in Skopelos town rise steeply from the wide quayside bordering the harbour. A long avenue of trees, whose tops are seen in the foreground, gives ample shade for a cool stroll.*
*Close at hand are many cafés and tavernas, to provide welcome refreshment for tourists.*

N

▲ 476

Ag.
Dimitrios

▲ 456

Kalamaki

Steni Vala

PERISTERA

Vrisitsa

Kokkinokastro

Alonissos

Chrisi Milia

Votsi
Patitiri

325

Vithisma
Marpounta

SKOPELOS

KYMI

# ALONISSOS

0          5 km

For legend see page 35

SIXTEEN

# Alonissos...and beyond

*Population: 1,554*    *Highest point: 476m*
*Area: 64 sq. kms*    *Hotel beds: about 500*

It is an exaggeration —though only just— to say that 25 years ago the people of Alonissos (Alonnisos) would not have recognised a tourist if one had arrived in their island! The concept of this island as a remote backwater is perpetuated even by those who should know better. As late as 1980 it was written that the port had no jetty, and that boats were used to offload the ferry. Another writer in the same year remarked that motor vehicles were virtually non-existent on Alonissos. Even then, both statements were untrue. The process of change continues —as with the recent arrival of a bus on the island, for instance.

The beginning can be pinpointed to 1965. At that time the great majority of islanders lived in a village 200m high on a hill overlooking the port. The village was called Alonissos, and the two tiny hamlets below, occupied with fishing and communication with the outside world, were Patitiri and Votsi. The only roads were mule tracks.

Then what looked like a major disaster struck, in the form of a terrible earthquake. All the houses in the village were damaged, and most became uninhabitable. The government acted, and a relief village was put up between Patitiri and Votsi where most of the villagers were rehoused. Others took the traditional opportunity of leaving the island to find work. Thus the stricken village found itself practically deserted.

Some Germans were first to take advantage of the situation. They began buying those empty and derelict houses which enjoyed such a magnificent view but were otherwise without facilities. With the money they received from these sales, and more spent by the new owners to restore them, some villagers found themselves with money in the bank. This they spent on materials to build themselves bigger and better houses, with extra space that they could rent to the growing number of summer visitors.

Meanwhile the government was spending further sums to improve the island infrastructure. By 1975 the breakwater had been extended, and a new jetty built for the ferry to berth. Throughout the island a framework of new motortracks was bulldozed. Today the situation prior to 1965 is reversed, and almost all the local people live around the port. In summer the old village is full of foreigners enjoying their holiday homes: in winter it is again deserted.

# Arrival by sea

The best way of reaching Alonissos is to fly to Skiathos airport and then make the short ferry trip across. Thus the arrival information in the chapter on Skiathos is relevant here. To summarise, the ferries are:

| From Volos | 8 - 12 sailings weekly | 5¼ hrs |
|---|---|---|
| | + 14 hydrofoil sailings | 2hrs 40mins |
| From Ag. Konstandinos | 1 +  sailings weekly | 5¼ hrs |
| | + 4 hydrofoil sailings | 2hrs 50mins |
| From Kimi | 1 - 3   sailings weekly | 2¾ hrs |
| From Skopelos | 7 sailings weekly | 35 mins |
| | + 19 hydrofoil sailings | |

During the peak summer season there is the slight chance of a weekly direct connection to Skiros.

# Centres of population

The boundaries between the three settlements in the port area are no longer obvious: the whole is at an early stage of becoming a small town, by island standards. The only tarmac roads in the island are within the port area, in and around which is found almost all the holiday accommodation.

With so many recently constructed buildings, the place has few pretensions to style, though bright and cheerful, and quite spaciously laid out. Shops are well stocked, and although overall choice is more limited, shops are comparable individually with those in Skiathos.

*Alonissos. The old village — seen here before the 1965 earthquake — was built high on a hill and fortified for potection against pirates. Tourists can now walk up to enjoy the sunset and marvellous views across the Aegean. The island offers some peaceful retreats, like the sheltered inlet below with its solitary dwelling.*

The ferry berths at Partitiri, in an inner cove of the bay lined with low cliffs, and sheltered from all except southerly gales. A number of cafés and restaurants line the waterfront. Ferry tickets for Loucas Nomicos are sold from a room on the ground floor of the Alkyon Hotel; the same room supplies banking facilities. Opposite is the petrol station, which also sells diesel. The island taxi usually waits beside the petrol station. There is a doctor, who keeps a supply of basic drugs, for at present the island has no pharmacy. (A trip across to Skopelos is quickly arranged, by caique if necessary.)

The old village is best reached on foot by the mule track, although there is now an alternative track for motors. On the way a number of circular stone threshing floors are passed — a reminder that quantities of wheat were once grown. The village has considerable atmosphere — a Tower of Babel during summer, but ghostly in winter. Immaculately reconstructed houses stand next to shattered hovels. For nearly two decades the new owners denied themselves such 20th century conveniences as electricity, but its recent arrival at the village shows they have overcome their scruples; piped water is expected to follow shortly.

## Accommodation

### Hotels

| Class | Name | | Rooms | Tel. (code 0424) |
|---|---|---|---|---|
| **At Patitiri** | | | | |
| B | Alkyon | (Pension) | 14 | 65430 |
| C | Galaxy | | 52 | 65251 |
| C | Alonissos Beach | | 45 | 65281 |
| **At Marpounta** | | | | |
| C | Marpounta | Bungalows | 104 | 65219 |

and 5 other lower category hotels.

**Private Rooms** There are a number of service apartments and, relative to size, many private rooms to let.

## Camping

Campers do come to the island, but are not welcomed with enthusiasm. Too many parts of the island have been devastated by forest fire, probably started by their carelessness. Nor are the beaches comfortable for sleeping on, unlike elsewhere in the Sporades. Water is relatively short, (although that is only a question of investing in more waterworks). Camping gas exchange bottles are unlikely to be found. There is the possibility of a future campsite at Steni Vala.

## Beaches and excursions

No tourist should come to Alonissos looking for established traditions or culture. The essence of this island lies in its unspoiled and unpolluted countryside and beaches. The interior, especially the higher ground, is superb for walking, but walking for its own sake, following a track to see where it leads, rather than aiming for a particular destination.

Even the beaches are not outstanding in themselves, but because of their fine settings. Trees often come right down to the water's edge, and partridge can be seen and heard in the woods behind. Above, piratical bands of the rare Eleanora's falcon lie in wait for the flocks of small migrating birds which use the islands of the Aegean as stepping stones. In the south several beaches are quite easily reached by motor track. Like most others, they are pebbles and shingle, with a rare patch of sand. Only at **Vritsa,** just north of the village and an ancient port, is there ample sand. Off **Kokkinokastro** can be seen, just under water, the remains of an ancient city.

**Steni Vala** is a popular destination for boat excursions, as well as being a starting point for boating and fishing activities. There is a tiny rocky inlet, with small hotel, a shop, and a good fish taverna. Beyond at **Kalamaki,** is another small hotel. These places could be reached by any car in good condition — at least in summer — but by boat is much easier. Further north the island is scarcely inhabited at all. Remains of another ancient city lie underwater at **Agios Dimitrios.**

## Historical background

We know that formerly there were at least two cities, so it is clear that the population of the island was once much greater than it is today, when villages suffice. Indeed like Skopelos, Alonissos once issued its own coinage. But there is a mystery. Alonissos often featured in Homer's legends: it was, for example, the home of Peleus, father of Achilles (whom we shall meet again on Skiros). But archeologists know that the name of the ancient submerged city at Kokkinokastro was Ikos. And we know from Strabo Ikos was capital of an island of the same name. So if today's Alonissos was Ikos, where is the ancient Alonissos?

## Peristera

The offlying island of Peristera was once joined to Alonissos. Later the whole east coast of Alonissos subsided: between the two islands there is now a sheltered stretch of water giving splendid opportunities for boating and sporting activities of all kinds (although its potential has scarcely begun to be exploited). Some of its fine sandy beaches are favourite destinations for boat excursions from Alonissos. The island has a tiny resident population of fishermen and shepherds.

## Kyra Panagia

The next island to the north is Kyra Panagia (Pelagos). It is beautifully fertile, well wooded, and entirely without permanent population. A wonderful choice for a desert (or at least deserted) island, on which to be cast away. There were once two monasteries, which remain intact but unoccupied. Since the whole island is owned by the church, change seems unlikely.

There are two excellent anchorages at the north and south ends of the island. At Agios Petros there are the underwater remains of an eleventh century Byzantine ship. The island has good beaches, and caves with stalactites. Some say one of these was the home of the legendary one-eyed giant Polyphemus, who used to amuse himself hurling boulders at passing ships. A species of wild goat, popularly called Kri-Kri, but more correctly Aegagos, is abundant.

## Yioura and Piperi

There is little that can be written about these two remote and uninhabited islands except that both are destinations for boat excursions from Alonissos. Yioura, where in fact it is prohibited to land, has a cave with perhaps a better claim than Pelagos to be the true home of the Cyclop, Polyphemus. Piperi is named after its resemblance to a pepperpot.

## Psathura

Furthest of all from Alonissos is the very remote Psathura. It is the site of a very powerful modern lighthouse. In recent millenia the island has become much smaller due to subsidence.

The boatmen of Alonissos may be reluctant to take you to Psathura. Distance may not be the only reason, for below the surface can sometimes be seen whole streets of houses, remains of another ancient city awaiting systematic exploration. The chances are that here lie the true remains of ancient Alonissos.

*Inlets at Votsi. These are popular with small boats when the adjoining harbour at Partitiri becomes congested with visiting vessels. In the background is the nearby island of Peristera. The south coast is well sheltered, and it is often easier to travel along it by water than by road.*

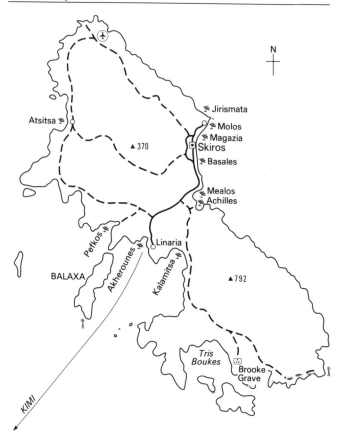

N

Jirismata

Molos

Magazia

Skiros

Basales

Mealos

Achilles

Atsitsa

▲ 370

Pefkos

Akherounes

Linaria

Kalamitsa

BALAXA

▲ 792

Tris
Boukes

Brooke
Grave

KIMI

# SKIROS

0       5 km

For legend see page 35

SEVENTEEN

# Skiros

*Population: 2,757*    *Highest point: 792m*
*Area: 209 sq. kms*    *Hotel beds: 67*

Skiros (Skyros) is distinctively different from the other inhabited islands of the Sporades, as well as being remote from them — fifty or more kilometres to the south east, and nearly as far from the mainland. It can only have been to suit the convenience of some administrator in the distant past that it was originally grouped with the rest. But whilst not typical of the Sporades, Skiros is a good example of an isolated Aegean island community, with all the problems that go with that.

To enjoy benefits similar to those on the mainland, an island must either be very close to it, or have a large population, or be rich in resources, or of vital strategic importance. Skiros is none of these, so as a consequence it has been losing population for the last hundred years or so. There was never a senior school on the island, so that the parents wanting their children to be fully educated had to move to Kimi or even Athens, often never to return. Clearly those who left would have been among the more ambitious and intelligent.

Island depopulation creates the converse problem of overpopulation in the cities, which successive governments have been slow to tackle. But during the early 1980s a new senior class was added to the school in successive years, until there is now a complete pre-university education available on the island. But other modern capital developments are few as yet, even for tourism, for which the island is quite well suited. Actually, quite large numbers of visitors do arrive during the summer, despite the slight provision made for them. Because of the very small amount of hotel accommodation, the great majority put up in private rooms, or camp out on the beaches.

## Arrival by air

A new airport has recently opened, to which a service from Athens
(daily in summer) is operated by the tiny Dornier 228 aircraft of
Olympic Airways. Flying time is 50 minutes. The airport is situated
on the north coast at a distance of 17kms from the Horio, to which
transport is provided (45mins).

*Displays of pottery dishes and copper ornaments typical of the
islands can be seen at the Faltaits Museum or, on a smaller
scale, in the model houses, where tourists can appreciate the
reconstruction of complete rooms in traditional style.*

## Arrival by sea

During the 1970s ferry schedules were tailored to suit the operational conveniences of Loucas Nomicos rather than the needs of the Skirians. In winter, for example, it could well happen that an islander needing to visit the mainland would have to wait a week for his return passage. So in 1980 this tightly knit community decided to do something about it; after much discussion they formed their own company, dipped deeply into their personal savings, and bought a ferry, the 'Anemoessa' which is now operated by the Skiros Shipping Company. Schedules are normally arranged to give at least a daily service to Kimi in each direction, which takes two hours: and since 'Anemoessa' is based on the island, usually departing in the morning and returning the same evening, islanders can visit the mainland without the necessity for an overnight stay.

'Anemoessa' was in ancient times the name of the island; aptly chosen, perhaps, since the meaning of the word is 'windy'!

After competing for several years Loucas Nomicos seems finally to have withdrawn its service to the island. At the time of writing there is no connection between Skiros and the North Sporades, except by transferring to the thrice weekly Loucas Nomicos service at Kimi. But it is quite possible that the North Sporades hydrofoil may develop to give a summertime direct extension between Alonnisos and Skiros.

## Road system

Before the advent of the airport, the only tarmac road was that linking the port to the town, where a small loop runs down to the beaches. It is rather narrow, and there can be difficulty in passing, but the amount of traffic using it is usually very low.

Unsurfaced secondary motor roads complete a figure of eight around the island. Their condition is mostly good.

**Buses** A bus meets the arrival and departure of each ferry, running from the town to the port and back. In the middle of the day a third bus trip is run. During the season, a second bus is pressed into service, and schedules adjusted to include the beaches. Administration is from Chalkis, in Euboea. Excursions have, in the past, been run round the island.

**Taxis** The island has no fewer than six taxis. When not in use, these will usually be waiting on the outskirts of the town, or at the port.
**Petrol** There is one station in the port, and another in the town, both of which sell diesel.

# Centres of population

The ferry berths at **Linaria,** a tiny sheltered port at the head of Kalamitsa Bay. The surroundings are picturesque, little more than a sandy cove, with a quay built out on the south side. A handful of shops, cafés, tavernas and ticket offices fringe the quayside. There are a number of little houses behind, where private lodgings can be found.

The capital, **Skiros** town, is known locally as the Horio. It lies on the opposite side of the island from the port, sheltering behind a massive rocky crag overlooking the sea. At the top of the rock is the Kastro: its present remains are Byzantine and Venetian. Just below in an impressive position stands the monastery of Agios Georgios (St. George) where a few of the town priests still live. Downward spirals a network of narrow twisting streets, into which, happily, motor vehicles can scarcely penetrate. Recent developments are situated on level ground at the edge of the old town, including the football field, which doubles as school playground and carpark. Banking facilities are found in the newspaper shop. Below the town is a large flat expanse of sandy land, fringed by wide beaches. Most of the island's rather slender tourist facilities are in this area. The remainder are on the two coasts, near to the road.

# Accommodation

### Hotels in Skyros

| Class | Name | | Rooms | Tel. (code 0222) |
|-------|------|--|-------|------------------|
| B | Xenia | Skyros beach (Magazia) | 22 | 91209 |

and two other lower category hotels.

**Private rooms** Many rooms are available in Skiros town and Linaria. Enquire at travel offices or watch out for 'To Let' notices.

# Camping

The island can afford to take a more relaxed attitude towards campers than the other Sporades, since the risk of fire is less. Camping in the vicinity of beaches is well tolerated by the authorities. Achilles beach, secluded but quite near the road, with a broad expanse of dunes behind, is particularly suited and naturists favour this area.

There is a small campsite on rented land just below the town, near the Xenia Hotel and some 200m from the beach. Facilities are rather simple but it serves, and improvements continue to be made.

Water taps and fountains are found all over the island. The water is good.

Camping Gas exchange bottles are unlikely to be found.

# The countryside

A saddle of low lying ground, along which the road runs, divides the island. On either side hills rise to a considerable height. The island can therefore be considered in two parts.

**The north of the island** This part is comparatively well wooded, although to a lesser extent than the North Sporades. In higher and more remote parts, away from the voracious attentions of marauding goats, a substantial area of pine forest supports a small resin tapping industry based on **Atsitsa.** The remains of copper mines can be seen.

There are also marble quarries — in the nineteenth century vast quantities of high grade marble were exported, which now embellish the capitals of Europe. One of these is near **Pefkos,** which also has an attractive beach. Indeed a number of sandy beaches, hardly used, can be found not far from the (unsurfaced) motor track which runs near much of the shoreline.

**The south of the island** This part is barren and stony. It is, however the home of a unique herd of wild Greek ponies. Once these were numbered in thousands: but today they are much diminished and, indeed, the tourist may have difficulty in finding any, although domesticated animals taken from the herd can be seen.

In the extreme south is the harbour of **Tris Boukes,** so called after its three entrance channels. In its time it was a superb anchorage for squadrons of battleships. Before that, it often served as a secluded lair for pirates, for whose activities the island was notorious. Today it is usually deserted, being deep and too exposed to gusting winds for the yachts that might wish to make use of it.

## Cultural background

To stroll through the streets of the **Horio** is a rewarding experience. At every hand there are reminders of the independent tradition and creative, artistic spirit of the Skirians. Costume continues to be worn as a matter of course by some of the older men. It was originally the working dress of the goatherds. Very loose baggy trousers of blue cotton are closed by black woollen gaiters. Unusual leather sandals are worn on the feet, which evolved to facilitate skipping nimbly along the rocky hillsides. Nowadays a cut out section of motor tyre is sometimes added to reinforce non-skid properties!

The most distinctive item worn every day by the women is a large yellow head scarf, printed with a traditional design in black. Under this the hair should be plaited in two pigtails. The skirts of festival dresses are remarkable, richly embroidered in traditional patterns.

Through the open doorways of houses can be glimpsed stylised arrangements of locally produced ornaments decorating the simple walls. Fortunately there are several 'model' houses which can be visited for a fee. Here can be admired at leisure hand carved furniture, copper dishes, ceramic plates, and embroidered pictures, most of which are produced in small workshops hidden away in the town.

The island is also rich in ancient customs which continue to be observed. Professor George Megas in his definitive Greek Calendar Customs makes possibly more reference to Skyros than to any other island. Thus on New Year's Day, when it is believed that St Basil comes down to earth and visits each house, a tray is set out with a bowl of water, two dishes of pancakes, a pomegranate and a pestle, so that St Basil may refresh himself and sweeten his tongue, and thus ensure that the house remain fresh and sweet all the year. On the same day the traditional "renewal of the waters" is combined with propitiation to the spirit of the well. After a church service "new water" is fetched to fill all the pitchers and jugs in the house, whilst at the same time figs, currants, nuts etc are thrown into the well, with the incantation "May all good things flow into our house with this water."

The last Sunday of Carnival, known as Cheese-Sunday, is observed with much feasting as elsewhere. But in Skyros it is believed that any person sneezing during the evening meal will not out-live the year; and so to prevent such evil fate, the sneezer's shirt is torn open from the throat to waist. There are also a number of special customs to be followed during harvesting, such as taking a wheatstalk from the first two sheaves and sticking it into one's belt, so that one's waist will not grow stiff from stooping.

**Museums** Just below Brooke Square are two small museums. The more interesting is called Faltaits, and is devoted to Skirian folklore. Its centrepoint is a splendid collection of seventeenth century embroidery. Open every morning except Tuesday.

**Festivals** The principal feast is at Carnival, immediately before Lent, when revelries with patently pagan origin, involving Bacchus and Dionysos, take place. On 23 April, the feast of St. George, Patron Saint of the Island, is also celebrated.

# Historical background

The Kastro was, in ancient times, an Acropolis — a defended area containing the most important religious buildings. The Odyssey has it that Achilles was brought here by his mother, to the court of King Lycomedes. The object was to keep him out of the Trojan War, to which end he was disguised as a girl: a fruitless ploy, since the crafty Odysseus found him out, and took him off to Troy to meet his fate.

Theseus, after he had lost power, retired to Skiros, which was already associated with Athens. But his enemies were vindictive. One day he was lured to the top of the Acropolis, and pushed off the edge to die on the rocks below. Later the Athenians were to change their attitude towards Theseus. During the Persian Wars, his ghost was seen fighting in the Athenian ranks. When this remarkable happening was reported to the Delphic Oracle, the Athenians were instructed to find Theseus's bones, and bring them back to Athens. An expedition under Kimon was hastily despatched to Skiros, where luckily the bones were discovered at the foot of the Acropolis, just where they had lain for hundreds of years!

Later Skiros became notorious for piracy. This was suppressed by Athens, and the island annexed. So many wealthy Athenians built themselves summer homes on the island that it was able to secure for itself tax free privileges. In spite of strengthening the fortifications, the Kastro was easily captured in 1538 by the infamous Barbarossa.

*Rupert Brooke's statue. The poet, cast in the heroic role of Greek athlete, gazes out to sea. Behind him is a point of land with traces of a primitive port; perhaps Jason and his Argonauts called here while on their way from Volos to the Black Sea.*

# Skiros and Rupert Brooke

As the Greeks warmed to Lord Byron, so the Skirians have adopted
as their own the English poet Rupert Brooke, who died at Skiros on
23 April 1915 (St. George's Day, note the coincidence). His statue
stands in a prominent part of the town, known as Brooke Square,
looking out to sea. The best way of getting to his grave presents the
tourist with a dilemma. It is possible to go by taxi, and be deposited
at the graveside. It's more romantic, and not much more expensive,
to take a boat from Linaria. There is a stone pier just to the south
of the riverbed: ten minutes walk up a track leads to the grave.
Finally it is possible to walk from Linaria, cutting across the beach
at Kalamitsa. A motor track then runs all the way to a lighthouse;
the final right turn towards the grave is marked by a small signpost.
(2½ hrs)

The Skirians will tell you that Brooke loved the island so well that
he expressed the wish in his will to be buried there. A charming tale
— and indeed Brooke's sonnet did anticipate his death abroad —
but the facts are otherwise. Brooke died of blood poisoning on
board the French hospital ship 'Dugay Trouin', which was then at
anchor in Tris Boukes. With the ship due to sail for Gallipoli next
morning, the burial took place that same evening, in an olive grove
convenient to the anchorage. The scene can perhaps be imagined.
The torches of sailors, flickering to illuminate the path. The stones
of the dried up river bed crunching beneath the pall-bearers' tread.
The sweet scent of blue flowering sage bushes. A hushed seclusion
in the deep shadows of the olive grove. So in a corner of this foreign
field was the poet laid to his final rest.

> If I should die, think only this of me:
>     That there's some corner of a foreign field
> That is forever England. There shall be
>     In that rich earth a richer dust concealed
> A dust whom England bore, shaped, made aware,
>     Gave, once, her flowers to love, her ways to roam
> A body of England's, breathing English air,
>     Washed by the rivers, blest by suns of home.
> And think, this heart, all evil shed away,
>     A pulse in the eternal mind, no less
>         Gives somewhere back the thoughts by England given;
> Her sights and sounds; dreams happy as her day;
>     And laughter, learnt of friends; and gentleness,
>         In hearts at peace, under an English heaven.

*The Soldier,* Rupert Brooke, 1914.

# Appendix A

## The Greek language

The main reason for including this chapter is that the effort of learning a few words of the language will be repaid many times by the reception you will get from the Greek people. Just to wish an islander "good morning" in his language is like paying him a compliment and although he may then assume that you speak fluent Greek and proceed to rattle on at top speed, you will be instantly accepted and liable to some of the very generous Greek hospitality.

Some of the smaller islands have very few English-speaking inhabitants and so a few of the most commonly used expressions may be helpful but a phrase book is a worthwhile investment and this chapter does not aim to replace them.

All Greek words in this book are spelt phonetically and not in the accepted English equivalent spelling. The syllable stress is very important in Greek and to put it in the wrong place can change the meaning completely. The accent denotes the syllable to be stressed.

## The alphabet

The Greek alphabet is confusing because some of the letters that look like ours have a totally different sound:

| | | | | | |
|---|---|---|---|---|---|
| A α | alpha | apple | Ξ ξ | ksee | rocks |
| B β | veta | never | O o | omikron | on |
| Γ γ | gamma | yellow or gap | Π π | pee | paper |
| Δ δ | thelta | then | P ρ | roe | roe |
| E ε | epsillon | enter | Σ σ | sigma | sand |
| Z ζ | zita | zip | T τ | taff | tiff |

| | | | | |
|---|---|---|---|---|
| H η | ita | ch**ee**se | Y υ ipsilon | pol**i**ce |
| Θ θ | thita | **th**ong | Φ φ fee | **f**end |
| I ι | iota | p**i**ck | X χ hee | lo**ch** |
| K κ | kappa | **k**ind | Ψ ψ psee | syna**pse** |
| Λ λ | lamda | **l**ink | Ω ω omega | **o**n (or owe |
| M μ | mee | **m**other | | at the end |
| N ν | nee | **n**ice | | of words) |

There are numerous letter combinations that make unpredictable sounds but this is rather off-putting for the beginner and so if you think you are ready for them, it is time to buy a teach yourself book.

## Some conversational gambits

Meanwhile, it is useful to be able to form a few elementary questions and make one or two simple statements. Apart from ensuring your basic survival and comfort when there is no one around who speaks English this will, as said before, create a really friendly rapport with the local people.

The following lists will help you to put a few simple sentences together. Of course, these will not be in grammatically perfect Greek (a language cannot be learned so easily) but if you say them carefully they should be comprehensible to any Greek person, who will be absolutely delighted by the effort you have made. Remember to stress the accented syllables.

### List A — basic statements and phrases

Yes: *neh*
No: *óhee*
Please/you are welcome: *parra kallóh*
Thank you: *efharistóe*
Good morning: *kallee máira*
Good evening: *kallee spáira*
Good night: *kallee níhta*
Hello/goodbye: *Yássoo* (*yássas* is more formal)
Greetings: *hyéretay*
Where is: *poo eénay*

I want: *thélloh*
I am: *éemay*
You are: *éesthay*
He/she is/there is/they are: *eenay*
We are: *ee már stay*
I have: *éhoe*
You have: *éhetay*
He/she/it has: *éhee*
We have: *éhoomay*
They have: *éhoon*
I don't want: *then thélloh*

Now if you turn to lists B, C and D you can add words to some of these to articulate your needs or ideas. Statements can be turned into questions by putting an intonation in your voice — to change "you are" to "are you?", for instance

## List B — accommodation

hotel: *ksennoe doheé oh*
room: *thomátteeoh*
house: *spéetee*
bathroom: *bányoh*
shower: *dóos*

bed: *krevártee*
hot: *zéstee*
cold: *kréeoh*
blanket: *koo vérta*

## List C — getting about

far: *makree áre*
near: *kondá*
bus: *leo for éeoh*
taxi: *taxí*
ferry boat: *férry bott*
street: *óh thos*
road: *dróh moss*
corner: *go neár*
left: *arist erráh*

right: *thex ee áh*
single: *applóh*
return: *epist rofée*
ticket: *ee sit ée ree ah*
post office: *tahee droh mée oh*
laundry: *plind éereeoh*
bank: *tráp ezza*
telephone: *telléfonoh*
petrol: *vrin zée nee*

## List D — eating and drinking

restaurant: *eest ee at ór ee oh*
food: *figh eet óh*
coffee: *kaféh*
tea: *ts ígh*
breakfast: *proh ee nóh*
sugar: *záh harree*

salt: *a lár tee*
pepper: *pip áir ee*
wine: *krass ée*
beer: *béerah*
water: *nair óh*
without: *hórris*
oil: *lárthee*

## List E — other useful phrases and words

As you gain a little confidence — and begin to understand the replies you get — you will probably be able to make use of the following phrases and words — when shopping, for instance. Note that, although days and numbers have been given here, it is more difficult to talk about time, such as the hours of boats and buses, so that is when you ask for it to be written down!

I want this: *thélloh aftóh*
I don't want this: *then thélloh aftóh*
What time does it leave?: *tee óra févyee*

What time does it arrive?: *tee óra ftáhnee*
Please write it down: *moo toh gráps etay parra kallóh*
Excuse me/sorry: *sig nóh mee*
I am an Englishman/woman: *éemay ángloss/angléeda*
Please speak slowly: *méelet ay argár parra kallóh*
Don't!: *mee!*
Go away!: *féev yet ay!*
Help!: *voh ée thee ah!*

Monday: *theftéra*
Tuesday: *tréetee*
Wednesday: *tetártee*
Thursday: *pémptee*
Friday: *parraskevée*
Saturday: *sávatoh*
Sunday: *kirree akée*

one: *énna*
two: *thé oh*
three: *trée ya*
four: *téssera*
five: *pénday*
six: *éxee*
seven: *eptá*
eight: *oktoé*
nine: *enay yáh*
ten: *théka*
eleven: *én theka*
twelve: *thó theka*
twenty: *ée cosee*
thirty: *tree ánda*
forty: *sarránda*

fifty: *pennínda*
sixty: *ex índa*
seventy: *ev tho mínda*
eighty: *ovthónda*
ninety: *en en índa*
one hundred: *eka tón*
two hundred: *thee ak ówsee ah*
three hundred: *track ówsee ah*
four hundred: *tétrak owsee ah*
five hundred: *pént ak owsee ah*
seven hundred: *eptak ówsee ah*
eight hundred: *okt ak ówsee ah*
nine hundred: *enyak ówsee ah*
thousand: *hill eeyá*

# Appendix B
## Wind Force: the Beaufort Scale*

| B'fort No. | Wind Descrip. | Effect on land | Effect on sea | Wind Speed knots | Wind Speed mph | Wind Speed kph | Wave height (m)† |
|---|---|---|---|---|---|---|---|
| 0 | Calm | Smoke rises vertically | Sea like a mirror | less than 1 | | | - |
| 1 | Light air | Direction shown by smoke but not by wind vane | Ripples with the appearance of scales; no foam crests | 1-3 | 1-3 | 1-2 | - |
| 2 | Light breeze | Wind felt on face; leaves rustle; wind vanes move | Small wavelets; crests do not break | 4-6 | 4-7 | 6-11 | 0.15-0.30 |
| 3 | Gentle breeze | Leaves and twigs in motion wind extends light flag | Large wavelets; crests begin to break; scattered white horses | 7-10 | 8-12 | 13-19 | 0.60-1.00 |
| 4 | Moderate breeze | Small branches move; dust and loose paper raised | Small waves, becoming longer; fairly frequent white horses | 11-16 | 13-18 | 21-29 | 1.00-1.50 |
| 5 | Fresh breeze | Small trees in leaf begin to sway | Moderate waves; many white horses; chance of some spray | 17-21 | 19-24 | 30-38 | 1.80-2.50 |
| 6 | Strong breeze | Large branches in motion; telegraph wires whistle | Large waves begin to form; white crests extensive; some spray | 22-27 | 25-31 | 40-50 | 3.00-4.00 |

| Force | Name | Description (land) | Description (sea) | | | | |
|---|---|---|---|---|---|---|---|
| 7 | Near gale | Whole trees in motion; difficult to walk against wind | Sea heaps up; white foam from breaking waves begins to be blown in streaks | 28-33 | 32-38 | 51-61 | 4.00-6.00 |
| 8 | Gale | Twigs break off trees; progress impeded | Moderately high waves; foam blown in well-marked streaks | 34-40 | 39-46 | 63-74 | 5.50-7.50 |
| 9 | Strong gale | Chimney pots and slates blown off | High waves; dense streaks of foam; wave crests begin to roll over; heavy spray | 41-47 | 47-54 | 75-86 | 7.00-9.75 |
| 10 | Storm | Trees uprooted; considerable structural damage | Very high waves, overhanging crests; dense white foam streaks; sea takes on white appearance; visibility affected | 48-56 | 66-63 | 88-100 | 9.00-12.50 |
| 11 | Violent storm | Widespread damage, seldom experienced in England | Exceptionally high waves; dense patches of foam; wave crests blown into froth; visibility affected | 57-65 | 64-75 | 101-110 | 11.30-16.00 |
| 12 | Hurricane | Winds of this force encountered only in Tropics | Air filled with foam & spray; visibility seriously affected | 65 + | 75 + | 120 + | 13.70 + |

* Introduced in 1805 by Sir Francis Beaufort (1774-1857) hydrographer to the Navy
† First figure indicates average height of waves; second figure indicates maximum height.

## Distance/Height

| feet | ft or m | metres |
|---|---|---|
| 3.281 | 1 | 0.305 |
| 6.562 | 2 | 0.610 |
| 9.843 | 3 | 0.914 |
| 13.123 | 4 | 1.219 |
| 16.404 | 5 | 1.524 |
| 19.685 | 6 | 8.829 |
| 22.966 | 7 | 2.134 |
| 26.247 | 8 | 2.438 |
| 29.528 | 9 | 2.743 |
| 32.808 | 10 | 3.048 |
| 65.617 | 20 | 8.096 |
| 82.081 | 25 | 7.620 |
| 164.05 | 50 | 15.25 |
| 328.1 | 100 | 30.5 |
| 3281. | 1000 | 305. |

## Weight

| pounds | kg or lb | kilograms |
|---|---|---|
| 2.205 | 1 | 0.454 |
| 4.409 | 2 | 0.907 |
| 8.819 | 4 | 1.814 |
| 13.228 | 6 | 2.722 |
| 17.637 | 8 | 3.629 |
| 22.046 | 10 | 4.536 |
| 44.093 | 20 | 9.072 |
| 55.116 | 25 | 11.340 |
| 110.231 | 50 | 22.680 |
| 220.462 | 100 | 45.359 |

**Distance**

| miles | km or mls | kilometres |
|-------|-----------|------------|
| 0.621 | 1 | 1.609 |
| 1.243 | 2 | 3.219 |
| 1.864 | 3 | 4.828 |
| 2.486 | 4 | 6.437 |
| 3.107 | 5 | 8.047 |
| 3.728 | 6 | 9.656 |
| 4.350 | 7 | 11.265 |
| 4.971 | 8 | 12.875 |
| 5.592 | 9 | 14.484 |
| 6.214 | 10 | 16.093 |
| 12.428 | 20 | 32.186 |
| 15.534 | 25 | 40.234 |
| 31.069 | 50 | 80.467 |
| 62.13 | 100 | 160.93 |
| 621.3 | 1000 | 1609.3 |

**Dress sizes**

| Size | bust/hip inches | bust/hip centimetres |
|------|-----------------|----------------------|
| 8 | 30/32 | 76/81 |
| 10 | 32/34 | 81/86 |
| 12 | 34/36 | 86/91 |
| 14 | 36/38 | 91/97 |
| 16 | 38/40 | 97/102 |
| 18 | 40/42 | 102/107 |
| 20 | 42/44 | 107/112 |
| 22 | 44/46 | 112/117 |
| 24 | 46/48 | 117/122 |

**Tyre pressure**

| lb per sq in | kg per sq cm |
|:---:|:---:|
| 14 | 0.984 |
| 16 | 1.125 |
| 18 | 1.266 |
| 20 | 1.406 |
| 22 | 1.547 |
| 24 | 1.687 |
| 26 | 1.828 |
| 28 | 1.969 |
| 30 | 2.109 |
| 40 | 2.812 |

**Temperature**

| centigrade | fahrenheit |
|:---:|:---:|
| 0 | 32 |
| 5 | 41 |
| 10 | 50 |
| 20 | 68 |
| 30 | 86 |
| 40 | 104 |
| 50 | 122 |
| 60 | 140 |
| 70 | 158 |
| 80 | 176 |
| 90 | 194 |
| 100 | 212 |

**Oven temperatures**

| Electric | Gas mark | Centigrade |
|:---:|:---:|:---:|
| 225 | ¼ | 110 |
| 250 | ½ | 130 |
| 275 | 1 | 140 |
| 300 | 2 | 150 |
| 325 | 3 | 170 |
| 350 | 4 | 180 |
| 375 | 5 | 190 |
| 400 | 6 | 200 |
| 425 | 7 | 220 |
| 450 | 8 | 230 |

**Your weight in kilos**

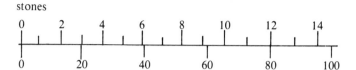

stones

kilograms

**Liquids**

| gallons | **gal or l** | litres |
|---|---|---|
| 0.220 | 1 | 4.546 |
| 0.440 | 2 | 9.092 |
| 0.880 | 4 | 18.184 |
| 1.320 | 6 | 27.276 |
| 1.760 | 8 | 36.368 |
| 2.200 | 10 | 45.460 |
| 4.400 | 20 | 90.919 |
| 5.500 | 25 | 113.649 |
| 10.999 | 50 | 227.298 |
| 21.998 | 100 | 454.596 |

**Some handy equivalents for self caterers**

| | | | |
|---|---|---|---|
| 1 oz | 25 g | 1 fluid ounce | 25 ml |
| 4 oz | 125 g | ¼ pt. (1 gill) | 142 ml |
| 8 oz | 250 g | ½ pt. | 284 ml |
| 1 lb | 500 g | ¾ pt. | 426 ml |
| 2.2 lb | 1 kilo | 1 pt. | 568 ml |
| | | 1¾ pints | 1 litre |

accommodation 56-8
  Agios Efstratios 138
  Alonissos 170
  Lemnos 126-7
  Samothraki 113
  Skiathos 146-8
  Skiros 178
  Skopelos 158-9
  Thassos 94
Agia Elenis (Skiathos) 149
Agios Dimitrios (Alonissos) 171
Agios Efstratios (island) 12,
  135-39
Agios Efstratios (village) 138
Agios Ioannis (church, Skopelos)
  164
Agios Konstandinos (port,
  mainland) 31
Agios Panteleimon (monastery,
  Thassos) 105
Agios Riginou (monastery,
  Skopelos) 164
Agios Sozon (monastery, Lemnos)
  134
Agnontas (Skopelos) 156, 160
agriculture and products 73-4
  Agios Efstratios 138
  Lemnos 129-31
  Samothraki 114
  Skiathos 150
  Skopelos 162
  Thassos 99
air services
  International 22-3
  to mainland ports 30-1
  Athens 53-5
  Lemnos 122
  Skiathos 142
  Skiros 176
Akhlades (Skiathos) 149
Alexandroupolis (port, mainland)
  30, 110
Aliki (Thassos) 98
Alonia (Samothraki) 112
Alonissos (island) 13, 166-72
antiquities, import and export
  of 119

Archangelou (monastery, Thassos)
  104
Aselinos (Skiathos) 149
Athens 44-55
  tourist information 14
Athens airport 23, 53-5
Athos, Mount 106-7
Atsitsa (Skiros) 179
Automobile and Touring Club of
  Greece 27
Avlonas (Lemnos) 128

Banana (Skiathos) 149
banks 67-8
beaches 74-5
  Agios Efstratios 139
  Alonissos 171
  Lemnos 128
  Samothraki 113-4
  Skiathos 148-9
  Skiros 179
  Skopelos 160
  Thassos 97-9
boat excursions
  Lemnos 134
  Skiathos 153
books 67
Bourtzi (Skiathos) 146, 149
breakdown service 27
Brooke, Rupert 183
buses
  Athens 46, 49, 50, 55
  international 25
  Lemnos 123
  to mainland ports 30-2
  Piraeus 53
  Samothraki 111
  Skiathos 145
  Skiros 177
  Skopelos 156
  Thassos 89

caiques 30
camping 57-8
camping contd.
  Alonissos 170
  Lemnos 128

Samothraki 113
 Skiathos 148
 Skiros 179
 Skopelos 160
 Thassos 95-7
car ferries see ferries
car hire 75
 Lemnos 124
cemeteries, Lemnos 125
Chora (Samothraki) 111-12
climate 17-19
coaches see buses
conversion tables 190-3
currency 67-8

Diapori (Lemnos) 129
distances 78
doctors 70
drama festival
 Thassos 104
drinks 61-2
driving to Greece 26-7

electricity 71
Elios (Skopelos) 160
entertainment 64
Episcopi (monastery, Skopelos)
 164
Evangelistria (monastery,
 Skiathos) 152-3
Evangilistria (monastery,
 Skopelos) 164
excursions 77
 Alonissos 171
 Lemnos 132-4
 Samothraki 117
 Skiathos 152-3
 Skopelos 163
 Thassos 104-7

ferries 28-43
 Agios Efstratios 136-7
 Alonissos 168
 inter-island 32-6
 international 25
 Lemnos 122-3
 mainland ports 22, 30-2

Samothraki 110-11
 Skiathos 142-3
 Skiros 177
 Skopelos 155-6
 table of mainland/island
  connections 38-43
 Thassos 86-8
 see also caiques, hydrofoils
festivities/festivals
 Skiathos 152
 Skiros 181
 Skopelos 163
 Thassos 104
fishing 64
 Lemnos 131, 134
food 59-61
fuel see petrol

Glisteri (Skopelos) 160
Glossa (Skopelos) 157
golf
 Skiathos 149
Greek language 184-87
Greek Travel Pages 14

health 70-1
Hephaestia (Lemnos) 128, 133
historical background 78-83
 Agios Efstratios 139
 Alonissos 171
 Lemnos 131-2
 Samothraki 114-17
 Skiathos 150
 Skiros 181
 Skopelos 162-3
 Thassos 101
Horio (Skiros) 178, 180
horse riding 149
hotels see accommodation
hydrofoils 29, 36, 143

Ipsarion, Mount (Thassos) 92

Kalamaki (Alonissos) 171
Kamariotisa (Samothraki) 112
Kaspakas (Lemnos) 128
Kastro (Skiathos) 149, 150, 153

Kastro (Thassos) 106
Kavala (port, mainland) 30, 86
Kavirio (Lemnos) 133
Key Travel Guide 14
Keramoti (port, mainland) 31, 86
Kimi (port, Euboea) 32
Kinyra (Thassos) 97
Klima (Skopelos) 162
Kokkinikastro (Alonissos) 171
Kolios (Skiathos) 149
Kontoupoli (Lemnos) 129
Kotsinas (Lemnos) 128, 133
Koukounaries (Skiathos) 148
Kremasta Nera (Samothraki) 117
Kyra Panagia (island) 172

Lalaria (Skiathos) 149
Lemnos (island) 12, 120-134
 seawater temperatures 19
Limenaria (Thassos) 91
Limenas/Limen (Thassos) 90-1,
 97, 103-4
Limonari (Skopelos) 160
Linaria (Skiros) 178
Loutraki (Skopelos) 155, 160

mainland departure ports 22,
 30-2
Makriammos (Thassos) 97
Mandraki (Skiathos) 149
maps 77
 Agios Efstratios 135
 air/sea transport links 33, 35
 Alonissos 166
 Athens 44, 47
 Lemnos 120
 Piraeus 51, 52
 Samothraki 108
 Skiathos 140
 Skiros 174
 Skopelos 154
 Thassos 84
 medical services 70
Megari Ammos (Skiathos) 149
Metamorphosis (monastery,
 Skopelos) 164
Milia (Skopelos) 160

monasteries
 Lemnos 134
 Skiathos 152-3
 Skiros 178
 Skopelos 163-4
 Thassos 104-6
moped/motorbike hire 76
motorways 26, 27
Moudros (Lemnos)125
museums
 Lemnos 124
 Samothraki 116
 Skiros 181
 Thassos 94, 104
Myrina (Lemnos) 124, 128, 134

National Tourist Organisation
 of Greece 14
newspapers 67
nudism 74

Pahia Amos (Samothraki) 114
Paleopolis (Samothraki) 112
Panagia (Thassos) 92
Panagia Kounistra (monastery,
 Skiathos) 152
Panormos (Skopelos) 160
Papadiamantis, Alexander 152
passports 16
Pefkari (Thassos) 98
Pefkos (Skiros) 179
Peristera (island) 172
petrol 27
 Alonissos 170
 Lemnos 124
 Samothraki 111
 Skiathos 145
 Skiros 178
 Skopelos 157
 Thassos 89
Piperi (island) 173
Piraeus 51-3
Platanias (Skiathos) 149
police (tourist) 16
Poliochni (Lemnos) 133
ports, mainland departure points
 to islands 22, 30-2

post offices 68
Potamia (Thassos) 92
Potamias, Bay of (Thassos) 97
Potos (Thassos) 98
Prodromos (monastery, Skopelos)
  164
products see agriculture and
  products
Profitis Ilias (Samothraki) 112
Psathura (island) 173
Psili Ammos (Thassos) 98

rail services
  Athens 49
  Athens underground 46
  to Greece 23
  to mainland ports 30-1
  Piraeus 53
rainfall chart 18
recreation 64-5
road signs 27
roads 75
  Agios Efstratios 137
  Alonissos 168
  to Greece 26-7
  Lemnos 123
  Samothraki 111
  Skiathos 145
  Skiros 177
  Skopelos 156
  Thassos 89
Samothraki (island) 12, 108-119
Samothraki (town) 111-12
sea transport see ferries
seals 139
seawater temperatures 19
Sedoukia (rock graves, Lemnos)
  164
shopping 66-7
Skala Prinos (Thassos) 86, 99
Skiathos (island) 13, 140-53
Skiathos (town) 145
Skiros (island) 13, 174-83
  rainfall chart 18
  temperature chart 17
Skiros (town) 178, 180
Skopelos (island) 13, 154-65

Skopelos (town) 155, 157
Sotir (Thassos) 92
sponges
  Lemnos 131
Sporades 12-13
sports 64-5, 74, 149
Stafilos Bay (Skopelos) 160
Steni Vala (Alonissos) 171

taxis
  Alonissos 170
  Athens 45
  Lemnos 124
  Samothraki 111
  Skiathos 145
  Skiros 178
  Skopelos 157
  Thassos 89
telephones 69
temperature chart 17
tennis 65, 149
Thanos (Lemnos) 129
Thassopoula (island) 107
Thassos (island) 12, 84-107
  rainfall chart 18
  temperature chart 17
Thassos town (Limenas/Limen)
  90-1, 97, 103-4
Theologos (Thassos) 92
Therma (Samothraki) 112
thermal springs
  Lemnos 134
Thessaloniki
  air services 23
time 78
tourist information 14
tourist police 16
Tripiti (Skopelos) 165
Tripiti (Thassos) 99
Tris Boukes (Skiros) 180
Troulos (Skiathos) 149
Tsimandria (Lemnos) 125
Tzanerias (Skiathos) 149

Velanio (Skopelos) 160
visas 16
Volos (port, mainland) 31
Vritsa (Alonissos) 171

walks see excursions
water 71
wind force chart 188-89

Xiropotamos (Samothraki) 112

Yioura (island) 172